The Women's Kama Sutra

The *Women's* *Kama Sutra*

THOMAS DUNNE BOOKS
ST. MARTIN'S PRESS ≈ NEW YORK

THOMAS DUNNE BOOKS
An Imprint of St. Martin's Press

The Women's Kama Sutra
Copyright © 2001 by Nitya Lacroix

For information, address:

St. Martin's Press,
175 Fifth Avenue,
New York,
N.Y. 10010.

ISBN 0 312 20627 5

First US Edition: June 2001

10 9 8 7 6 5 4 3 2 1

Contents

Introduction 6

On the Arts of Pleasure, Sensuality and Love 16

Sexual Compatibility 46

Astrological Compatibility..72

The Importance of Physical Affection 84

The Kama Sutra Arts of Love 120

Erotic Acts...142

Transcendental Sexuality 168

Introduction

"The purpose of *The Women's Kama Sutra*
is to celebrate female sexuality
and its untold potential for pleasure,
ecstasy and transformation."

When that wonderful classic work of Hindu erotic literature The *Kama Sutra of Vatsyayana* was first published widely in the West, readers were shocked by the explicit detail and diversity of its sexual information. They were astounded by the elaborate and complicated sexual positions described, and intrigued by the bold, uncensored approach that it took towards the subject of sexuality.

The book reached popular mass attention in the West during the 1960s, at a time when a sexual revolution was emerging after a long period of puritanism. In particular, Western women were beginning to reclaim their power in making choices about their sexuality. The advent of the contraceptive pill freed many women from the burden of fear of unwanted pregnancies, while the work of leading American sex researchers, such as Dr Alfred Kinsey in the 1950s and William Masters and Virginia Johnson in the early 1960s, had scientifically proven that women were sexual beings in their own right, and were not sexually compliant purely to fulfil their roles as wives and mothers. Masters and Johnson's studies revealed that the female orgasmic response followed a very similar physiological pattern to that of men, that the clitoris is as erotogenic an organ as the penis, and that women have the potential to be not just orgasmic, but multi-orgasmic too. Suddenly, a new ray of light was shone on female sexuality. The ignorance about this issue, which for centuries had deemed women's sexuality to be inferior to men's, began to be dispelled. Now the

onus was on men to improve their sexual technique, and women began to expect and demand that their orgasmic potential and sexual happiness be satisfied. Women were no longer content to be purely the passive partner, doomed only to the submissive and inert "missionary position." Now they had permission to express themselves sexually, sometimes taking the assertive role in lovemaking, and to be uninhibited about their passion. Nor were women prepared to remain content with the "three minute" sex act that Kinsey had reported as the norm of the married couple. The word was out – women were sexual beings, and the nature of their sexuality was orgasmic and ecstatic. Hence the *Kama Sutra* suddenly had mass appeal, for it not only detailed a variety of exciting and erotic sexual positions, it did so without guilt. Moreover, this ancient work addressed the importance of a woman's sexual happiness. It understood her orgasmic process, and clearly stated her sexual equality with men.

This awareness of female sexuality, which arrived late to Western consciousness, was always inherent in Eastern thought. In India, where society generally disapproves of overt displays of physical affection, there has been historically a wealth of testimony to the joys of eroticism. Thus, *The Kama Sutra of Vatsyayana*, which is believed to have been compiled about the 4th century AD, burst upon a Western audience that was incredulous but hungry for new sources of enlightened erotic information.

The *Kama Sutra* was compiled by the sage Vatsyayana from a number of ancient texts written

over centuries by Hindu scholars relating to sexual matters. The word *Kama* can be translated as sensual pleasure, eroticism, love and desire. The word *Sutra* refers to the style of prose, which is a short aphorism or teaching instruction. The pursuit of *Kama*, or the sensual and sexual pleasures of life, was not viewed as a decadent indulgence; it was one of the three principal goals of life through which a person could attain the fourth and ultimate goal, *Moksha*, which is the liberation of the mind and

The Kama Sutra *portrays women as sensual and sexual beings in their own right and who are able to initiate and take control in the arts of lovemaking.*

spirit, and therefore enlightenment and the freedom from the cycle of rebirth.

It is worth trying to understand the purpose of these goals, and examining briefly their relevance to the life of a woman today.

Dharma

Dharma means 'truth', and it refers to the pursuit of both a spiritual and moral life according to the scriptures and the natural law. This was considered to be the most important of the three goals, for without it a person could lack judgment and responsibility. Women have a natural sense of moral law, even if they do not abide by any particular convention or religion. They have always tended to be the natural nurturers and carers of the family, discharging their responsibilities to others without selfishness. Even today, when women are working in full-time careers, they seldom neglect their duties at home or the needs of their loved ones. Many modern women are interested in personal growth and development, seeking ways to be more open and honest with themselves and others, and to improve the quality of their relationships.

Artha

Artha is the pursuit of wealth and material well-being. This goal may be a well-established one in contemporary society, but it is rarely regarded in a spiritual context as it was in the Hindu teaching. There it was seen as the duty of a citizen to provide financial security for his family, for poverty would lock him into the concerns of basic survival and thus prevent his contemplation of other-worldly and higher matters.

A woman in our age must also pay attention to her financial situation. She can no longer rely on the fortunes of a father or husband, and she must prove herself in the marketplace as equal to a man. Financial independence is an important goal for women because it gives them freedom and choice at all stages of their lives. These days, a woman has to be capable of earning her living because she may choose to stay single and want a carefree lifestyle that she can afford; she may be divorced or widowed and bringing up children on her own; she may need to share the mortgage and household costs with her partner; and she must be confident that as she grows older she can do so with grace and independence.

Choosing the right career or means of supporting herself is always an important decision, and it should be one that not only covers her material needs, but also allows for creative expression and personal satisfaction.

Kama

Kama is the pursuit of sensual pleasure and desire, the search for the fulfilment of our senses and sexuality. The word *Kama* is taken from the name of the Hindu god of Love and Desire, who is a similar deity to Eros or Cupid of classical mythology. No one, not even the mighty gods of the Hindu Pantheon, could resist the erotic power of his blossomed arrows once they had pierced the heart. All would become bewitched by love and desire for the first person upon whom their eyes fell.

The goal of *Kama*, according to Hindu teaching, is not simply the pursuit of hedonism. It is the cele-

bration of the senses which, according to the *Kama Sutra*, are the windows of the soul. It is the honouring of the body as the temple of the spirit, and of human sexuality as a gateway to the Divine. The sexual act of the man and woman, according to the ancient tradition of Hindu Tantra, a spiritual philosophy of India, was symbolic of the union of the male and female principles of Cosmic Conscious-

Thomas Cantrell Dugdale's Nude. *The ancient Hindu texts taught that feminine sexuality was divine and urged men to honour and worship the female body as a gateway to inner transformation.*

ness. In that state of Absolute Bliss all dualities merge, and harmony pervades the whole of Existence. When the male and female principles separate from that union, the female energy becomes a cosmic force, manifesting in every aspect of creation.

The principle of *Kama*, therefore, requires a woman to always respect her body and take great care of its well-being, regardless of her other duties. She should feel comfortable with and proud of her sexuality and her natural sensuality, and learn the ways in which they can bring her great pleasure and joy. *Kama* is the essence of women.

Celebrating the sexual act

The philosophies of Tantra, which are further explained in Chapter Seven, and on which the goal of *Kama* are based, never divide the body from the soul, nor the sexuality from the spirit. All are aspects of divine creation, and the means through which both men and women can reclaim their divinity. Hindu art reflects this in its visual celebration of the erotic. Throughout India, there are sculptures and artworks that portray the sexual act as sacred. Temple and cave carvings depict explicit acts of human copulation. These symbolize more than man's age-old homage to fertility, for they are images of human sexuality as a microcosm of the great mystery of Cosmic Creation.

Throughout this book, the human genitalia are frequently referred to by their Hindu Tantric names. The *lingam* is the male phallus, the penis.

The *yoni* is the female vulva. In India, the symbol of *lingam* and *yoni* is carved in stone or wood and found in temples and places of worship throughout the country. It represents the sacred sexual union of the Tantric god, Siva, and his consort, Shakti, which forms the divine principle of Cosmic Consciousness. By their act of merging in sexual ecstasy, all universal duality is dissolved. When Shakti separates from her Lord, she is the sexual energy of Creation. All women are, therefore, a personification of Shakti energy, and their sexuality must be revered.

The Kama Sutra of Vatsyayana was originally written as a social guide for the aristocratic societies of India. Its instructions mainly addressed the privileged and indolent young men of the higher castes of Hindu society. It is full of advice which, in an egalitarian culture of a different age, would be considered elitist and snobbish. Yet the *Kama Sutra* never ignored the sexual needs of women, and it taught the men to be skilful and sensitive lovers. It had plenty to say about courtship and romance, and how to create a sensual ambience for love.

It is often assumed that the *Kama Sutra* concerned itself purely with erotica, but this is far from the truth. Its contents also focused on the accomplishment of social, recreational and household skills that were befitting to the life of a noble citizen. It had advice too for the courtesans who kept

Ritual yoni vessel. Erotic carvings depicting female genitalia, known as the 'yoni', are common symbols of worship in India.

company with such men, and for the citizen's wives who remained at home.

The *Kama Sutra* stated that women had much to gain from studying its 64 arts and sciences. Vatsyayana argued that women instinctively understood these practices, suggesting that even young maids should study these arts and sciences, "with the consent of their husbands." In doing so, he said, wives gained independence and would be able to support themselves in times of need.

The feminine perspective

The Woman's Kama Sutra focuses specifically on the issues of sensuality and sexuality detailed by Vatsyayana, but looks at them from a feminine perspective, and in ways that are relevant for the contemporary woman. It draws from the text of the *Kama Sutra,* which was translated from Sanskrit by Sir Richard Burton, the Victorian explorer, and which was first published in 1883. Due to its explicit sexual material, the book was privately published and sold at that time by an organization called the Kama Sastra Society, which had been specifically set up to translate and study the classic texts of Eastern erotic literature.

The purpose of *The Woman's Kama Sutra* is to celebrate female sexuality and its untold potential for pleasure, ecstasy and transformation. In an age when a woman has more choices then ever before, she should feel confident and skilled in the arts of love so that the choices she does make are the right ones.

Finally, we live in an age where we have greater sexual freedom than in previous times, but with that comes extra responsibility. The *Kama Sutra* teaches that human sexuality should be engaged in without guilt, but it should be entered into with a consciousness of love and awareness. We must treat ourselves and our partners with respect. We must also educate ourselves on all sexual matters and their consequences. For the woman that means taking good advice about contraception if she does not wish to become pregnant. It is imperative for both sexes to take precautions against transmitting or becoming infected with sexually transmitted diseases. At a time when HIV/AIDS and other venereal diseases are prevalent in the population, it is essential to use condoms for protection or to engage in safer sex practices which prevent the exchange of body fluids, except within the context of a monogamous relationship where the sexual health status and history of both partners can be absolutely guaranteed. Health centres and hospitals should carry the necessary literature to inform you of all of these issues.

Ritual linga or phallus. Phallic sculptures in wood or stone represent the god Shiva, who embodies the male principle of cosmic consciousness.

CHAPTER ONE

On the Arts of Pleasure, Sensuality and Love

" A female, therefore, should learn the *Kama Sutra*, or at least a part of it, by studying its practice from some confidential friend. "

The *Kama Sutra* is a philosophy on the love of life. It is the gospel of pleasure and sensuality – a testament to celebrating physical and earthly happiness without guilt or censure – and is a perfect teaching for women who wish to explore the potential of their sexuality and to live joyfully.

As the original teachings of the *Kama Sutra* were written from a masculine perspective, and primarily addressed an aristocratic society in which men were held in higher esteem than women, a contemporary woman may ask how the teachings of the *Kama Sutra* are relevant to her life. Women now are more liberated than their sisters of that bygone time. They have greater access to equality in work and law, and they are more in charge of their lives. A woman, however, must now compete alongside men in a world still largely defined by men. She is also often the principal carer within her family and her life may be filled with responsibility. Yet a woman needs to seek the balance between duty and joy in her life and to remind herself that she is still an innately sensual and sexual being who is worthy of love. *The Women's Kama Sutra* explores the female experience of pleasure and sensuality, and though it draws from the teachings of an ancient time, much of that wisdom can be interpreted as relevant to a woman's quest today for fulfilment and happiness.

> **" Kama is the enjoyment of appropriate objects by the five senses of hearing, feeling seeing, tasting and smelling, assisted by the mind together with the soul. "**

The five senses

It is through your five physical senses that you are able to experience and enjoy the tangible energy and creativity of life. The senses are the doorways to delight and pleasure upon which the whole principle of *Kama* is based. When your five senses are fully heightened, you feel alive and vital and in touch with all that surrounds you. Your love of life, your sensuality and your sexuality are all enhanced by the full involvement of your senses.

In today's world, the many demands made upon one's time and the constant bombardment of noise and the stimulus may result in the senses becoming dulled. If this is the case, it may take a little extra effort to regain for yourself a more acute sensory awareness so that you become receptive and responsive, thus participating more fully in the pleasures of life. Devote time to each of your senses, focusing on each one in turn.

Hearing

Seek solitude and peace away from all preventable and intrusive noises. Close your eyes, relax your body and sink your consciousness into the silence, focusing only on the quiet inhalation and exhalation of your breath. Remain like this for up to 15 minutes. Transfer your attention to any natural external noises. Can you hear the wind rustle in the trees, the song of a bird, the patter of rain? Isolate that sound in your mind and let it fill your awareness.

Introduce harmonious sound into your environment, creating a more melodic influence within your home territory. Place wind chimes in your garden so that a passing breeze will set off their gentle music. The bubbling sound of a small water feature in your garden will also have a relaxing effect on you and on those who share your hospitality. Play music at home as you carry out your domestic tasks and when you relax. Let the sound fill you, move you and inspire you.

Expand your appreciation and understanding of all kinds of music, listening to everything from classical to jazz, opera to modern pop. Attend concerts and festivals with friends so that music becomes the milieu through which to socialize and meet new people.

Learn to be a good listener, hearing the words your loved ones speak to you, and allowing yourself time to comprehend the feeling and emotions behind them before you react or respond.

Touch

Feeling is connected with your sense of touch, the physical contact that is made between you and that which surrounds you. Touch is the function of your skin, which contains thousands of sensory nerve endings that transmit their sensations to your brain.

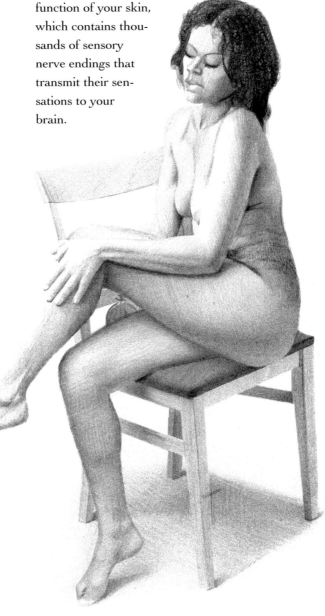

Kama is the enjoyment of appropriate objects by the five senses of hearing, feeling, seeing, tasting, and smelling, assisted by the mind together with the soul.

As you touch, and are touched, so you form the sense of yourself in relation to the outside world. This sense more than any other confirms your relationship to the whole of existence. The loving touch you received from your parents in childhood established your feelings of self value. Through reaching out and touching others, you open and share your inner self and your world of feelings to those around you.

Let your touch be vibrant and warm. Do not be afraid to take the hand of a friend in need, or to show your concern or affection by holding a loved one close in your arms. When you place your hand on another's body, do so with full attention and presence of mind.

Develop your sensitivity of touch by bringing your awareness into your hands, noting the shape, texture and feel of objects with which they come into contact. Become more tactile and you will become more alive to your feelings. Feel the tender softness of a newly unfurled leaf, the warm body of a cat or the delicacy of silk, and become aware of your responses to that contact.

Develop a whole-body sense of touch by enjoying massage, and by sensitizing your skin through self-massage and anointing your body with lotions and essential oils.

Be physically affectionate to your partner even at times when sex is not on the agenda. When making love, touch and stroke your lover's whole body and do not neglect any part of him. Encourage him to be as sensual and tactile with you. Become submerged in the different responses of your body as you are caressed in return.

Seeing

Whenever it is possible, gaze on this world with a softened focus. Allow your sight to become receptive so that you absorb into yourself the wondrous details of the natural beauty that surrounds you. Stop and look at a flower, a tree, the clouds, a sunset or the moon. If you live in a city, seek out any aspects of nature which continue to exist in the environment. Seize the opportunities to leave behind you the cluttered skylines and artificial lights, so you can allow your sight time to adjust to the expansive horizons of an ocean, an open landscape or a starlit sky.

Each day, look at your lover with fresh eyes, without projecting the events of the past on to the person before you. When you talk to each other, never dominate each other with your eyes, but let them be receptive and welcoming to the person you love. Do not be afraid to let your eyes reflect the warm feelings in your heart, for a caring look can bring great comfort to another person.

Make eye contact with your partner when you make love and let your innermost feelings of passion and love shine through your eyes. In moments of intimacy, let go of your individual egos and allow your eyes to meet and absorb each other on the deepest levels of being.

Feeding morsels of succulent foods such as exotic fruits and chocolate to your lover can become an erotic act because taste is a sense that stimulates sexual arousal.

Taste

During the Tantric sexual rituals of ancient India, a man and woman would exchange offerings of food to each other. These were usually items of food and drink normally forbidden by the scriptures of the Holy Law. Through their devotion and prayer to the god and goddess, the tantrikas believed that their offerings assumed a divine substance. Taste is experienced through those most sensual of body parts, your mouth and tongue. Little wonder, then, that good food and drink are so often associated with sexual arousal.

Develop a connoisseur's taste for the good things in life, so that you celebrate eating and drinking with friends or with your beloved. Savour all the different taste sensations by carefully selecting and preparing what you eat so that you truly appreciate the fullness of its flavour. Avoid dulling your taste buds by smoking cigarettes or adding too much spice or condiments when you cook. Ensure your diet has plenty of natural, healthy and organic foods which do not contain artificial flavourings or chemicals. Present your meals with the eye of an artist, balancing the colours of the meal and arranging it beautifully on the platter, and prepare your table with fine plates and crockery. All these preparations will heighten your sense of taste. Feel gratitude for your food and eat it slowly, chewing each mouthful carefully and with awareness, and ensuring that you do not overeat. Learn the art of choosing fine wines to accompany your meals, sipping your drink slowly in order to appreciate fully its aroma and flavour.

Play a sensual taste game with your lover. Prepare a tray on which you set out a variety of delicious morsels of food, such as small pieces of mango, peach, strawberries, coconut, cream cheese and chocolate. Try to arrange a varied and exotic array of flavours. Pour some of your favourite beverages into small glasses, selecting from choices such as liqueurs, champagne, wine or fruit juice. Put a blindfold on your lover or cover his eyes with a silk scarf so he cannot guess what titbit you will feed him. By removing his visual sense, his consciousness of taste will be heightened. Offer him these treats piece by piece, allowing him time to savour each succulent flavour. On another occasion, let him prepare a taste ritual for you to indulge in.

Some lovers enjoy combining the sense of taste with the sense of touch in an erotic game. Your partner can spread certain delicious foods such as chocolate, cream, honey or the pulp of an exotic fruit on to your bare skin. Slowly and sensually, he can lick the edible substance from your naked body, using his tongue and lips to sexually arouse you. On another occasion, you can return the favour to him.

When you make love, gain a sense of your lover's own unique taste. Kiss, lick, suck and nibble each part of him as if you were feasting upon his body.

Smell

The sense of smell can have a profound effect on your moods and can certainly play a powerful role in attracting love and romance into your life. Smell affects the part of your brain that governs emotion and memory. Odours can attract or repel you, lift your spirits, act as an aphrodisiac and relax or stimulate your mind. Perfumes have long been used in religious and sexual rituals to create an aromatic ambience for the elevation of the spiritual and physical senses. The Hindu texts of ancient times frequently refer to the use of potent scents, such as camphor and sandalwood, during sacred ceremonies and tantric sexual rituals.

It is well known that sexual scents, known as pheromones, are emitted from the sex glands of certain animal species and play a primary part in their mating behaviour. Some of these animal sexual scents, such as musk, have traditionally been added to perfumes for their aphrodisiac effect on human beings. It is also believed, although not yet scientifically proven, that men and women produce their own sexual pheromones which operate on a subliminal level to attract the opposite sex. It is highly possible that you are instinctively attracted to a man because of his bodily smell without being conscious of the fact. One of the tricks employed by certain women, wise in the secrets of love, is to dab a touch of their own vaginal juices behind their ears to act as a subtle aphrodisiac perfume.

When you prepare and cook food, let your sense of smell guide you as much as your sense of taste. Smell influences taste, and an aromatic dish will increase your appetite and taste delicious.

Choose plants for your garden not only because of their colour, but on the basis of their fragrance. Vary the sweet perfume of flowers with the refreshing or pungent smell of herbs and bushes. Take pleasure in inhaling the aroma of nature's bounty, breathing in the perfume slowly and with full awareness. When you go for a walk, stop to smell a rose, a bed of lavender, freshly mown grass, or the fresh breeze of an ocean. Close your eyes to focus fully on this wonderful olfactory stimulation. Take note of how these smells can alter your mood.

In Tantric ritual, smell is the sense associated with the awakening of sexual energy. When you make love, do so in a room subtly perfumed with essential oils of aphrodisiac qualities. When you make love, smell each other's bodies and rejoice in the earthy, musky sexual odours without inhibition.

Using aromatic essences

Throughout its text, the *Kama Sutra* refers to the use of perfume for creating an ambient mood that will heighten sensual and sexual experiences. Among the pleasure-seeking aristocracy of ancient India, fragrances from plants and flowers such as sandalwood and jasmine were blended into pastes, oils and powders and applied to the body for both cosmetic and aphrodisiac purposes. Sweetly scented flowers were gathered and woven into garlands that were placed in the hair or used to adorn opulent rooms where potential lovers were cordially entertained.

The art of using aromatic essences has regained its popularity in contemporary society, and now, thanks to the wide range of good-quality essential oils currently available in pharmacies and health shops, it is easy to create your own evocative and fragrant potions for health, beauty, home, sensual massage and sexual pleasure.

Essential oils are the essences of flowers, leaves and roots from plants, herbs and trees, which are distilled or abstracted from the plant by various means depending on the country of their origin and on the composition of their chemistry. Essential oils possess different therapeutic properties which can assist healing in the body, emotions and spirit. More importantly, for the purposes of sensual massage and lovemaking, the aromas of these essential oils can have a profound effect on the part of the brain which influences mood and memory. Below is a guide to some of the essential oils which can be used to create the right mood for the appropriate occasion. Once blended correctly, so that their perfumes are harmonized, they can be used in aromaburners to fragrance the environment, in lotions for beauty treatments, or mixed into basic vegetable oils for sensual massage and lovemaking. Once they are blended, store your oils in dark-tinted glass bottles and keep them away from the glare of direct sunlight.

Essential oils are potent substances, and it is important that you understand the effects of their properties and educate yourself on their contraindications. Once informed, invite these natural essences into your life to help you engender an atmosphere of relaxation, stimulation, openness and love for your home and for the harmony of your body, mind and soul. Be guided by those fragrances which appeal specifically to you and your partner.

"The outer room, balmy with rich perfumes, should contain a bed, soft and agreeable to the sight."

Stimulating oils

Some essential oils bring warmth and a touch of spice to your aromatic blends, awakening the senses and revitalizing sexual energy. These essences have been used since antiquity for aphrodisiac purposes, in addition to warming and easing tense muscles, boosting the blood circulation and generally stimulating the physical responses of the body. Such spicy essences include basil, ginger, and black pepper. Orange will put a touch of zest and vitality into your mix, while stimulating juniper will evoke erotic feelings.

Erotic oils

Certain floral essences seem to epitomize the spirit of *Kama*, for not only are they intensely erotic, they also influence sexual healing. A few drops of sweet, heady ylang-ylang in your blend will create a seductive mood, opening the heart and increasing the libido. Ylang-ylang is also reported to heal male impotence and female frigidity.

The divine perfume of rose absolute, extracted form the delicate rose petal, is indeed a heavenly fragrance created in the spirit of love. It promotes sweet, tender feelings and, acting as an aphrodisiac, awakens love and sexual energy. It is reputed to aid in the healing of past emotional hurts, helping lovers to let go of painful memories and reopen their hearts to love. Jasmine absolute is an essential oil whose exotic perfume has long been enjoyed by lovers and newlyweds in countries such as India. Its character is warm and erotic, instilling a sense of confidence and self-esteem, and its use is thought to relieve the psychological causes of sexual tension.

Evocative oils

Woody essential oils, drawn from bark or sap, can be added to an aphrodisiac blend to create an atmosphere condusive to spiritual elevation and meditation, and to help lovers focus on the present moment.

These essences are evocative in nature and their inclusion in a sensual massage oil blend will initiate emotional and spiritual communication. Sandalwood, whose use in lovemaking rituals is mentioned frequently in the *Kama Sutra* and in Tantric texts,

The delicate fragrance of an aromatic blend of essential oils added to your bath water will relax your mind, elevate your mood and pamper your skin.

encourages physical sensuality and emotional honesty. Cedarwood essence, with its wonderful deep woody smell, helps to banish sexual anxieties and, like the haunting aromas of frankincense, can elevate spiritual consciousness.

Relaxing oils

The presence of healing lavender essential oil in a blend will impart a sense of calm, relaxing the body and soothing the mind. Bitter-sweet neroli absolute, distilled from delicate orange blossom, is both an aphrodisiac essence, used for its powers of seduction, and a relaxant. Sweet geranium initiates harmony and balance between the male and female energies, and intoxicating clary sage calms sexual fears and outward stress, dissolving inhibitions and boosting libido.

Women in particular have an affinity for the power of aromatherapy because they have a natural desire to create a sensual and healing environment around themselves. If you wish to gain a better knowledge about the properties and effects of these aromatic essences, and to learn how to make remedies and recipes of the correction dilutions, you can gain this information from books or courses dedicated to the art and science of aromatherapy.

Beauty comes from within

A woman's true sensuality and beauty develop from her relationship with her own body, and her self-esteem. It is an internal process through which she must discover what feels pleasing and comfortable to herself, which she must then nurture for her own sake. A woman who tries too hard to emulate an image imposed from the outside may feel as if she will never succeed in becoming attractive to others.

> **"She should be possessed of beauty and amiability, with auspicious body marks."**

The fashionable norm for idealized beauty changes constantly throughout the ages, and from one culture to another, but these fashions are artificial standards which belie the individual potential of each woman. Whether the current trend for female beauty is based on the ideal of a voluptuous or a slender figure, a blonde or brunette, each woman must endeavour to love and appreciate her physical appearance for its own particular uniqueness. Although it is quite natural for a woman to desire the admiration of men, or of her friends, for the way she looks, she should not be driven by others' expectations, the pressures of fashion trends or an image-conscious media. To do so leads to a neurotic state of mind and a debilitating lack of self-confidence.

The daily rituals of physical care encourage a woman to develop a healthy body image.

A healthy lifestyle

Health and fitness are the foundation of beauty and vitality; it is the sense of well-being in body and mind that illuminates your physical appearance. Take responsibility for establishing a routine of good eating habits and daily exercise which will boost your state of health and create in you an aura of wholeness and vivacity. Approach these projects in a enthusiastic way, but not with fanaticism, because if you become obsessional about matters of health and fitness this in turn will cause tension and self-obsession.

Weight is an issue that preoccupies most women. If this fact is true for you, then put aside your concerns about losing weight or going on a crash diet and begin to create a happy relationship with food. Educate yourself on the nutritional properties of food, and establish a routine of eating regular and balanced meals. Your diet should be based on a wide variety of foods and should contain ample supplies of fruit and vegetables, wholegrains, and a selection of low-fat proteins and unsaturated fats to provide you with the necessary intake of vitamins and minerals, fibre, calories, and amino acids which you require for health and vitality. A balanced and nutritious diet helps your skin, hair, and nails to remain in good condition and feeds your energy and vitality. Remember to follow the tip of the top fashion icons and drink plenty of fresh water throughout the day too, for this will aid the digestion and the elimination of toxins from your body, encouraging a clear and healthy glow in your complexion.

A regular exercise routine such as yoga enhances the body's muscle tone and flexibility while bringing equilibrium to mind and spirit.

Avoid using food as a replacement for love or as a way of easing boredom or the ache of loneliness. Be courageous enough to face up to the underlying issues of your unhappiness, and seek alternative methods of transforming negative feelings into positive actions.

Keeping fit

A woman at ease in her body vibrates a special kind of attractiveness. If you feel fit and flexible, if your muscle tone is good and your stamina levels are high, you will display a confidence in your movement and demeanour which friends will admire and men will find appealing. Exercise is important because it enables you to absorb more oxygen into your lungs so that your cells and tissues are nourished and your heart and circulatory system stay healthy. Walking, swimming, running, playing sports, and working out in the gym will encourage better muscle tone, and fluidity and co-ordination of movement.

Explore the exercise systems that have their roots in the ancient East, such as yoga, t'ai chi or martial arts, for they work more profoundly to create equilibrium in body, mind, and soul. Their practise will bring strength and flexibility to your physical form and will also help you to focus your mind and harness your emotions.

> " Now, the householder, having got up in the morning and performed his necessary duties, should wash his teeth, apply a limited quantity of ointments and perfumes to his body, and put some ornaments on his person. "

Looking after your body

The young Hindu men to whom the *Kama Sutra* predominantly addressed its advice were obviously the peacocks of their society. Social etiquette demanded that these aristocratic studs preened and pampered themselves in ways which would certainly raise eyebrows in most circles today. In modern society the emphasis on beauty care falls to women, although a reasonable degree of masculine self-care, hygiene and body care never goes amiss.

Caring for your body should be a daily ritual. The extra attention and touch involved will increase your sensuality. Rise a little earlier each morning to enjoy a lengthy shower and to have time to attend to some aspect of body care.

Routines of sensuous beauty

• At least three times a week, exfoliate your skin with a dry brush or loofah before your shower. Circle the brush up over your limbs and torso towards the direction of your heart. This will remove the dead cells from the outer layer of your skin, aiding its elimination of toxins. The brisk motion will enliven the skin's sensory nerve endings and boost the blood circulation towards its surface so that your whole body feels vibrant and soft to the touch.

*Bathing in the sacred rivers is an important element of spiritual
life in India.*

• As the pressure of the water massages your body, especially your shoulders and neck, take pleasure in its liquid caress on your skin. Once you have soaped yourself all over, slide your hands over your whole body, gliding them sensuously over your breasts, thighs, belly and buttocks.

• Hair that is clean, bouncy and shining will give you an air of confidence, drawing the eyes of admirers. Shampoo and condition your hair regularly, carefully selecting the correct cosmetic products for your particular hair type. As you wash you hair, briskly and thoroughly circle your fingertips over your scalp to ease away tension from the head and to stimulate the blood flow to the hair follicles. This will have an invigorating effect on your mind as well as improving the condition and shine of your hair.

• After your morning shower, apply skin-nourishing lotion, cream or oil to your body, using the opportunity to self-massage and relax your muscles. Sit on a stool and press and squeeze your feet to boost your whole nervous system, knead your calf muscles to ease away tension, and pummel your thighs rapidly with loose fists to increase the circulation and to help dispel any build-up of cellulite in the tissues. Use similar motions to lubricate and relax your hands and arms. Spread the lotion over your buttocks and hips and smoothly circle your hands clockwise over your abdomen. Attend lovingly to your breasts, for this most feminine part of you deserves your special attention. Rub more moisturizing cream on to the palms of your hands and glide them softly over the fullness of your breasts, and then on to your ribcage and shoulders.

Daily face care

While a woman cannot prevent the natural process of ageing, she can do much to preserve her youthful complexion by looking after her skin. Every morning and evening, attend to the beauty care of your face, cleansing and moisturizing the skin without fail. First of all, know your skin type, and select your cleansing cream and moisturizer accordingly. Create your own cosmetic recipes by adding a few drops of a skin-nurturing essential oil to a lotion. By cleansing regularly you can counteract the detrimental effects of environmental pollution, and by avoiding too much exposure to the sun you can prevent its harsh, drying effects on your skin.

Gentle massage

When you apply your moisturizer, use the opportunity to massage your face gently so that it regains a relaxed and open appearance. Anxiety and stress create tension in your face muscles, hardening your features and presenting to the world a mask-like countenance. Soften your features by exercising your face muscles, pulling funny faces at yourself in the mirror, widening your eyes and opening and pursing your mouth. Then remove the tension with your fingertips, circling them over your jawline and cheeks. Soothe your brow with smooth circular strokes, moving from the centre of your forehead and outwards, so that you complete the massage with gentle anti-clockwise strokes over your temples. Using the palms of your hands, spread the moisturizer down over your neck. Now gently but vigorously tap and vibrate your fingertips over your face so that you boost the circulation to the skin, creating a radiant and healthy glow.

Soft hands and feet

Take good care of your hands and feet so that they remain soft and well-presented, for these small details are noticed by others and add greatly to your aura of beauty. Protect your hands from the harsh effects of hot water and detergents by wearing rubber gloves when you do your household chores. Apply ample moisturizing creams and lotions to your hands and feet on a daily basis, and massage them well to keep them supple and soft to the touch. You can mix one or two drops of essential oil to your lotion to nurture and fragrance the skin. Lavender or patchouli will help to heal rough, dry skin, while rose absolute or neroli will leave behind a lingering and exotic fragrance. Manicure your nails regularly so their appearance is smooth, clean and elegant. Beautiful hands and feet are sexy, and never more so than when they reach out to touch a lover's skin.

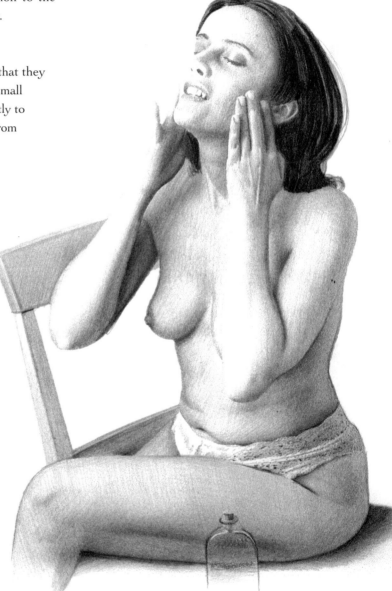

Moisturise your face daily with nourishing lotions and use your fingertips to massage away tension.

Female eroticism

A woman's whole body is erogenous, capable of responding with delight to the caresses of her lover. Yet a woman can also awaken her own orgasmic potential so that she understands her body's own secret desires. Through sensual self-masturbation, you can experiment with the type of touch and stimulation which gives you the greatest sexual satisfaction. Plan an evening alone and bathe in a warm bath perfumed with relaxing and sensual aromatic oils. Relax each part of your body as you soak in the water and consciously let go of stressful thoughts.

After the bath, dry your body and spread a moisturizing cream over your skin. Enter your bedroom, which you have prepared beforehand so that it feels warm, romantic and welcoming, and lie naked on your bed. Start by lovingly stroking every area of your body. Run your fingers softly over your face, gliding them tenderly over your features. Move your hands slowly down your body, exploring its form, shape and texture – the swell of your breasts, the softness of your belly, the brush of your pubic hair, and the warm, wet depths of your vagina. Let your fingers search out your clitoris, stroking and stimulating it gently so that you can feel its erotic sensations radiating outwards into your vulva and pelvic floor. Take your time to enjoy each new sexual feeling. Experiment with different rhythms of movement, sometimes slow and occasionally rapid, but take care not to hasten too quickly towards an orgasm. Breathe deeply into your pelvic area and down towards your genitals so that your body remains relaxed. You can touch and stimulate your anus and

By engaging in autoeroticism, a woman can explore her sensual responses. She can discover what kind of caress can bring her pleasure, leading her to a satisfying orgasm.

33

perineum and stroke and pull gently on your pubic mound. Spread your vaginal juices over your clitoris, and let your body move and rock with pleasure. The whole purpose of this exercise is to explore your many different physical responses. If you wish, you can allow fantasy to increase your arousal, but you can also choose to remain completely attentive to your erotic feelings. Eventually, let yourself reach the threshold of orgasm, discovering exactly which caresses bring you to its height and subsequent release. Abandon yourself to the sensations of orgasm, lettings its pulsation move through the whole of your body.

> **"She should keep the whole house well cleaned, and arrange flowers of various kinds in different parts of it."**

Exercising the pelvic floor muscles

The *Kama Sutra* refers to the "mare's position," a sexual position during which *"the woman forcibly holds in her yoni the lingam after it is in . . ."* and adds that this activity is learned only by practice. Strengthening your pelvic floor muscles may help you to gain better control over your vaginal muscles during intercourse, which can add to your own and your partner's pleasure. Pelvic floor exercises may benefit your orgasmic potential too, because they stimulate the blood circulation to this area and build up the tone in the muscles. The exercises are quite simple and should be practised daily; they can be done anywhere and take only a few minutes to complete.

Try to isolate the pelvic floor muscles. To do this, wait until you are urinating, and then contract your muscles to stop the flow. Then relax. Having achieved this, you now know which sets of muscles to work. First, in a standing, sitting or lying position, contract these muscles, holding for a count of three, then relax them and repeat the exercise once. Next, contract and release the muscles rapidly up to ten times. Then slowly pull the muscles upwards as if you were sucking up with your vagina and hold the contraction for a count of three before releasing. Finally, bear down on this area as if you were pushing the muscles into your vagina. Relax after three seconds.

Home is a temple of love

In the era of the *Kama Sutra*, the citizen's home was his milieu for seduction; everything within it was arranged for the pursuit and indulgence of pleasure. According to the text, the aristocratic citizen was expected to obtain his wealth by inheritance or gift, and then live the life of a good householder in a city, a large village or a place which was a popular social resort. His home was luxurious, preferably close to water, and surrounded by gardens. Within the home were many

The Kama Sutra *urged prospective lovers to create within the home a romantic ambience that was conducive to seduction.*

rooms, some of which would be possibly occupied by his harem of women. The house was fragranced with pots of perfumes and vases of flowers, and littered with toys and games to occupy the householder's idle days.

Into this home, the citizen would invite a woman that he desired and practise his arts of seduction. He would entertain her in the pleasure room which was adorned with flowers and filled with exotic perfumes, and attended by his circle of friends. They would pass the time in conversation, play games, sing and listen to musical instruments, eat and drink. Once his female guest became relaxed and enamoured of her host, the party of friends would disappear. Then, utilizing his great skill in the arts of love, the citizen would slowly begin to make love to the woman. When their sexual intercourse was over, the man would continue to dedicate his attention to the woman. He would massage her with pure sandalwood ointment and embrace her, offer her food and deserts, and drinks such as sherbet, mango juice or sweetened citrus. Then he would lead her to the porch, and in the moonlight the woman would lie in his lap while the citizen explained to her the mysteries of the stars.

Clearly, from the description of the above scenario, the elite males of this era lived like kings within their home environment, and had an army of servants at hand to tend to all the domestic tasks. Rich and unhampered by the need to work, they could create a princely environment in which to indulge their fantasies and pleasures.

Few of us today could hope to live in such opu-lent homes, enjoying such indolent and luxurious lives. However, while you may not own the ultimate house of your dreams, you can still create a home environment which welcomes romance, love and friendship. You should feel like a queen within your own home, so let it become a place where you can express your personality, your aspirations, and your creativity. This is where you can relax and play, and where you have the freedom to act out your desires away from the eyes and judgments of others.

The pleasure dome

Transform your home, however humble or opulent, into a pleasure dome which is your refuge and sanctuary. With some imagination and the appropriate materials, you can create an environment which is an open invitation to romance and love.

Ensure your home is well ventilated, allowing in fresh air every day to dispel stale odours. Fragrance your rooms with aromatic essential oils burnt in an aromaburner, or bowls of perfumed pot pourri, scented candles or vases of sweet-smelling flowers. Be careful, however, not to overwhelm your olfactory sense with too many conflicting perfumes, but let the fragrance be subtle, uplifting and deeply sensual.

Arrange your home so that it is pleasing and restful to the eye. Throw out the clutter of your past which is no longer meaningful to you so as to create an empty space where the new may enter. Let there be a central point within each room on which your gaze can focus, such as a candle or a statue, a hearth fire or an array of flowers.

A temple of love

Select decor, materials and fabrics in colours which relax and inspire you, and visually influence your moods. Tantric colours such as red, orange and terracotta are associated with sexual awakening, and imbue a room with a feeling of warmth and sensuality. They are an exotic choice for your chamber of love. Shades of blue relax and soothe you, and can inspire meaningful communication between yourself, friends and a beloved. Green is the colour that resonates with the heart and kindles love, while yellow hues cheer and brighten your spirits. Lilac, pink and mauve are soft and feminine colours, inducing feelings of sentiment and romance, while the purity of white conveys cleanliness, simplicity and emptiness.

Place cushions and pillows of soft fabrics in the room where you and your partner intend to make love. Do not feel that you must confine your sexual relationship to your bedroom, but prepare the room of your choice beautifully, so that it is fragrantly scented and softly lit and becomes a temple for your acts of love.

Turn your bedroom into a sanctuary of love, decorating it with luxurious fabrics that are sensual to touch and lie on. The Tantric colours of red and orange encourage sexual arousal.

Making love in your bathtub may be restricted by its size, but if the mood takes you, and you have room to manoeuvre, then it can become a very romantic and sexy occasion. If it is night-time, soften the room with the glow of candlelight. Prepare your soaps and lotions beforehand, and have warmed, clean towels ready for use. Fill your bath with hot water and add to it up to seven drops of aphrodisiac, relaxing or evocative essential oils, choosing from a selection of not more than three essences, such as jasmine, sandalwood, neroli, patchouli, ylang-ylang, rose, lavender and frankincense. Make sure that you thoroughly agitate the water to disperse the essence within it.

Soak together with your lover, stroking and massaging each other's bodies. Arouse each other gently. The most comfortable sexual position you can assume in the limited space of a bathtub is the female superior one. Kneel or squat astride your partner's thighs so that you can carefully lower yourself on to his member. This can be done either facing him or with your back turned to him, both of which provide him with a visually stimulating view of your body.

Creating a social life

The social life to which the *Kama Sutra* referred was active and varied. Many of the recreations mentioned could be easily transposed into the social diaries of today's seekers of romance and pleasure, for they included parties, festivals and picnics, drinking and eating, gambling, conversing, swimming, engaging in sports, and listening to music. Other activities appear quaint, or even faintly alarming: *"After breakfast, par-*

rots and other birds should be taught to speak, and the fighting of cocks, quails, and rams should follow."

During the sultry days and nights in the lush country terrain, young men and women held festivals to celebrate the advent of spring, ate the exotic and delicious mango fruits, held picnics in the forests and even pelted each other with tree blossoms.

The women who engaged in these activities were known as "public women", and were actually courtesans. They were not family members or female friends, who would have had no opportunity to socialize freely, but rather women who were trained in the arts and sciences of love and pleasure. These women were educated in many skills and particularly in the ability to entertain men in the ways of mind and body. These courtesans were not thought of as common prostitutes. Although they lived outside the strict moral rules laid down by the scriptures and the conventional standards of their time, they were held in a particular kind of regard and played an important role in the social life of Hindu society. In fact, a considerable part of the *Kama Sutra* is dedicated to advising these courtesans on social behaviour, how to win a rich and handsome lover, ways to obtain money and possessions and, finally, on methods to get rid of an unwanted lover.

Today, the social scene is completely different for women. Most women have the right to mix freely in the company of their choice, and to express themselves sexually as they wish. A woman can enjoy the friendship of men, she can work alongside them, join them in sports, and choose her relationships without censure or criticism. This freedom, however, does not mean that it is easy for the modern woman to find the right partner for herself; she may have to become creative with her social life to meet new and exciting men to whom she is attracted, and must balance the demands of her career with her desire for pleasure and love. At certain periods of her life she may wish to experiment with different relationships without becoming seriously attached to anyone. Then there may come a time when she wants to settle into a committed relationship, when she must seek a man who shares her long-term aims.

One thing is certain – the modern Western woman rarely has a relationship arranged for her, so she must seek love for herself and take her chances. Without a strict structure of moral law around her, she must set her own boundaries and conditions. She has to create her own opportunities for love to happen.

Looking for love

If you are looking for love and romance, it is pointless sitting at home alone waiting for a knight in shining armour to charge through your door and carry you away. Take charge and seek love in a positive, but not needy, way. Present yourself in an attractive fashion at all times. Work on your confidence and self-esteem, but be open and sensitive to others.

If your work does not provide you with a social outlet, seek the company of others during evenings and at weekends. Invite friends to your home and

Dancing with the man you feel attracted to will quickly reveal if your bodies are rhythmically suited.

cook them dinner, occasionally asking one friend to bring along an acquaintance who is known to them but not to you. In this way, you are networking and constantly expanding your social circle. One positive contact can always lead to another.

Enrol in societies, clubs, classes or workshops which encourage activities that interest you and that you are fond of, and you may meet a kindred spirit. If you enjoy physical activities, join a sports and leisure club that is equally welcoming to men and women.

Ask your closest girlfriends to introduce you to potentially suitable partners. They know your character and preferences, and if they are loyal to you, they will assist you in your search for happiness. Always nurture your friendships with other women, for they will be there for you in both good and bad times.

Take a complete break from your normal routine to encourage the more spontaneous side of your nature, so that you may meet and relate to people in a fresh and responsive way. Take a holiday, go abroad, have a weekend break and – although you should always exercise reasonable caution about your personal safety – stay open to the possibility of a romantic adventure.

Let your heart be filled with love whatever your romantic state. Love manifests itself in many ways, not only in a sexual manner. Let it be there in friendships, among your family, in your feeling for animals and nature, or in the passing smile of a stranger. Love can happen at the most unexpected times, but it will be drawn to you by the openness of your heart.

On wooing

Wooing a lover in the era of the *Kama Sutra* was an elaborate affair, filled with etiquette and cunning art. The man was expected to be skilled at courtship, winning over a female's affection by compliments and attention. If she was young and inexperienced, he brought her gifts, persuaded her to meet him in secret, and tried to amuse her in every way with game and conversation. Once he had gained her confidence, and was secure about her feelings for him, he slowly began his seduction. Careful not to rush his advances or frighten the young women, he sat near her at parties and gatherings and indicated his desire through his brief tender touches, his behaviour and his body language. He would whisper secrets to the girl and she would be convinced that she alone was special to him. Only when he was sure that the girl was completely smitten by him would the man proceed with his sexual advances.

According to the *Kama Sutra*, a young woman was supposed to be equally cunning in her efforts to gain a husband. When she met a man suitable to her desires, she should plot to meet him privately and as frequently as possible, give him gifts of flowers and perfume and show him her skills in

> **"A girl always shows her love by outward signs and actions."**

A confident modern woman should feel free to signal her attraction to the man she admires.

massage and the arts. She should engage him in conversation, steering the topic around to the subject of love – though the *Kama Sutra* insisted that the female should never initiate a sexual advance, for this caused her to lose respect in the eyes of others. Instead, she should respond to her suitor's declarations of love, but resist his attempts to become more sexually intimate. Only when the girl was convinced of his love and of his desire to marry her could she relinquish her virginity.

Changing times

These traditional rules for wooing and courtship were fairly well defined until relatively recent times. Women were supposed to be coquettish and demure, and although well aware of their effect on men, they were the guardians of sexual virtue. While the woman, through her actions, could subtly signal her attraction, it befell the man to initiate the first overtures of courtship and gain her affection. He might make manly attempts to seduce her, but he was expected to accept her resistance. The woman was out to seek a husband and gain her respectable place in society, and the man wanted his bride to be a virgin or at least, known only by him.

Good eye contact and a relaxed open posture extend a welcoming invitation for further contact.

Times have changed, and the acceptable standards of gender behaviour have mostly been turned on their heads. Women are more assertive, and some men are afraid to be chivalrous for fear of feminist derision. Women enjoy a greater freedom to express themselves sexually, and certainly many will experience several sexual relationships before making a commitment to one man. Virginity is no longer a female prerequisite for marriage, although society still maintains some double standards in favour of men in regards to moral behaviour.

The changes in traditional gender roles can make the process of wooing an awkward and disappointing one for a women. A woman may rightly demand an equal status to men, yet she wants her femininity acknowledged too; while she may insist on her rights, she wants to be wooed as well.

The dance of courtship

The nature of courtship is like that of a dance, for it has a mysterious rhythm of its own. It is a shifting energy played back and forth between the man and woman, and its pleasure rests in a balance of power which is held alternately by each of them. You may want to be straightforward with your thoughts, feelings and desires when you first meet a new man, but practice some discretion – too much directness at this

stage could act as a sledgehammer on a delicate moment or on the masculine ego.

When you first meet a man who attracts you, neither demur to him nor try to overpower him with your intellect, personality or sexuality. Let him discover who you are slowly, revealing only so much of yourself as is worthy to the situation. Do not engage in a battle of egos, for you have nothing to prove. Be true to yourself, be confident, and avoid creating a false impression of yourself.

If you have spent some time at a social event trying to attract the attention of a man and he fails to respond to you in a satisfactory way, leave him alone and seek the company of another person. When you show your interest in someone to no avail, avoid wasting your precious time. If, however, you are unsure of his feelings for you, you can attempt to get a mutual friend to find out discreetly.

> **She never looks at the man in the face, and becomes abashed when she is looked at by him; under some pretext or other she shows her limbs to him.**

Body language

When the chemistry is right between yourself and a man, let your body do the talking because it has a language of its own. You are unlikely to be as bashful as the young girl described above in the *Kama Sutra* text, but your actions will probably be just as revealing. Do make eye contact, but don't be afraid to display some signs of shyness. Lean a little forward towards him, so that your body reveals an eagerness to become more familiar. If the attraction is strongly sexual, then you may find that you wet your lips with your tongue occasionally. Folding your arms across your chest will indicate that you are protecting yourself and send the wrong messages, so allow your body to remain open and relaxed.

The first touches

In the initial stages of wooing the first physical contact should be tentative and subtle, with parts of your bodies brushing together as if by accident. These are important moments to be aware of, because you can gauge by this contact whether or not your attraction is real. From these small beginnings, great pleasure and passion can develop.

According to the *Kama Sutra*, when the woman bends down in front of the man to whom she is attracted and covertly brushes her breasts again him, this is known as a "piercing embrace." The text goes on to say that these types of physical contact are only likely to take place between people who are not yet familiar to each other.

Placing your hand on your new friend's knee or shoulder is another way of breaking the

The first light brush of the lovers' bodies is called the 'touching embrace' in the Kama Sutra.

ice to make an initial physical contact. Rest your hand on his body lightly, so that your touch feels attentive but not needy. Holding hands as you take your first walks together can encourage intimacy in the earliest stages of courting. Dancing closely together, body to body, is an excellent way to sense each other's rhythms and to know if you share a real physical compatibility. If your movements are harmonious, it can feel as if you are making love.

When to make love

The *Kama Sutra* recommends that wooing and courtship should be relished for its own sake before a couple decide to make love. It insists that a woman needs time to trust the situation and gain the respect of the man. It is for every woman to decide for herself whether that is just old-fashioned nonsense or plain words of wisdom.

> **"When a man under some pretext or other goes in front of or alongside a woman and touches her body with his own, it is called the "touching embrace".**

What is certain is that you should never let yourself be pressured into making love in a new relationship before you feel ready. You must judge for yourself when the time is right. If you enter the situation with a clear awareness that your body, mind and soul are willing, then you are probably ready. There is a beauty in waiting until intimacy, trust and passion have developed between yourself and the man. The body can be impulsive, but there are many other factors to be taken into account. You must agree on issues of safe sex practises and contraception, and you should try to be honest with yourself about what you want from this sexual encounter.

A man who knows how to court you like a queen is a king of the *Kama Sutra* arts of love. A man who has patience to wait and woo the women he loves is the man worth waiting for.

CHAPTER TWO

Sexual Compatibility

> " Men and women
> being of the same nature
> feel the same kind of pleasure,
> and therefore a man
> should marry such a woman
> as will love him ever afterward. "

Many factors are at play when a woman and man are initially attracted to each other, but the real success of the relationship depends on the couple's ongoing mental, emotional and sexual compatibility. The word "compatibility" is defined as the ability to relate or live together harmoniously and, like many aspects of life, it is an organic state which is capable of undergoing change and growth.

Initial attraction

That powerful first rush of energy that happens in sexual attraction is exciting and exhilarating. It is an instinctive response to our animal bodies, and both the woman and man are most probably drawn to each other because they are transmitting a similar level of sexual vibration. There is a special chemistry at work between them, and when it happens it feels like magic. This attraction exerts a magnetic pull between the two people which is usually highly charged on an emotional and sexual level. Such passion acts as the fire of love, opening up their bodies, hearts and minds.

Indiscriminate Passion

Instant sexual attraction, however, is by no means an infallible guide to relationship compatibility. It is impossible to know the whole person when you first meet someone – indeed, it is unlikely that you even know all aspects of yourself.

Passion can be indiscriminate in its choices, and sexual attraction is often fuelled by unconscious forces. A woman may be drawn to a man because he appears to represent something she longs for in a partner; perhaps strength, virility, protectiveness, or status. A man may be attracted to the woman because of her beauty, image, femininity, and personality. Both people may project on to each other qualities of character which belong more to their own subconscious fantasies than to the object of their desire.

The overwhelming of the senses in the first heat of a passionate affair is intoxicating and can override many other considerations. It is all too easy to miss those early signs of incompatibility, both intellectual and sexual, which may exert a negative influence on the relationship at a later stage. Women in particular have a tendency to overlook potential areas of incompatibility when they are first engaged in the emotions of love and sexuality; they may be primarily involved in their feelings for their lover rather than concerned with the realities of the relationship.

A woman may also believe that the strength of her love alone is sufficient to change her partner, or the relationship for the better. This is a grave mistake. People change only when they are ready to and want to, and no one else has the power to exert those changes, even though love can sometimes provide the milieu in which a process of transformation may happen.

The Kama Sutra *teaches that sexual compatibility is essential for a happy love life or marriage. A couple should be well matched physically and share a comparable sexual appetite.*

Assessing your relationship

The old saying "love is blind" has its truths. When a woman is seeking an enduring relationship she should endeavour to look at her love situation with unblinkered eyes. She must assess whether her relationship has the material within it to provide a strong foundation for the future, instead of believing that she has the power, and the right, to change another person to suit her needs. While every human being has the possibility for transformation and growth, it is a foolish woman who believes that she alone holds the key to unlocking her lover's potential. A woman must take responsibility for her choices of relationship, no matter how much she is in love or in the thrall of sexual passion. Eventually she must judge the situation honestly and ask herself if there is enough common ground to build a relationship which is sufficiently compatible and flexible to allow for the continued growth of love and mutual respect.

Both women and men must pass through the many varied and often unpredictable events of life. Circumstances change us, age and experience alter our attitudes and values. Certain events bring out our strengths, other situations expose our vulnerabilities. A sexual relationship is unlikely to maintain its same high level of initial intensity, and different emotional and physical factors will influence our sexual needs. Therefore, in addition to compatibility, a successful relationship requires acceptance, tolerance, and adaptability if it is to continue to survive happily.

Achieving Sexual Compatibility

If you want close sexual intimacy and trust to grow between yourself and your partner, you should be willing to discuss your lovemaking issues and to share your needs and desires. As the woman, you may discover that your man is initially reluctant to talk about feelings, so you need to encourage this kind of sharing carefully and sensitively. Generally, men have fragile egos when it comes to their sexual performance. Criticism of his sexual performance is counter-productive, and can create a defensiveness from which it is hard to recover. Encouragement, humour, praise, and talking honestly about what turns either of you on, or off, will help to keep your sexual relationship responsive and compatible.

Exploring the new

Be willing to experiment and explore with different ways of making love so that you do not fall into a monotonous pattern. If either of you has had previous sexual partners, your current relationship can benefit from the knowledge gained from your past experiences. However, it would be a mistake to presume that what worked for you with a past lover will automatically suit your new partner. Be open to the new and let your sexual relationship unfold naturally, allowing you to discover an unexplored landscape of delight.

Vulnerable feelings can be safely exposed when a relationship is built on intimacy, trust and honesty.

Compatibility develops from taking the time to know one another properly. Everybody has their own unique sexuality, and it may take a little time for you and your partner to become attuned. Hug, cuddle, kiss, caress, and enjoy extended periods of foreplay because it is through these intimate activities that you will begin to know and respond to each other intimately on a physical and emotional level. Learn to massage each other so that you become sensitive, loving, and familiar to the other's body without the immediate rush towards intercourse.

It is quite natural for a woman especially to need to feel secure and trusting in her relationship before she is completely able to open up sexually. It is important to remember that true sexual compatibility between a man and woman has its foundation primarily in their love and regard for each other.

Different but Equal

The difference in the ways of working, by which men are the actors and women are the persons acted upon, is owing to the nature of the male and female.

The teachings of the *Kama Sutra* reinforce the wisdoms of the Taoist and Tantric texts in perceiving male and female sexuality as different but equal. Vatsyayana, who compiled and commented on the texts which formed the *Kama Sutra*, believed that men and women brought separate and distinctive qualities to lovemaking and while each possessed a different sexual consciousness they ultimately drew the same degree of pleasure from it.

In his view, the man was the active principle of lovemaking and the woman was the passive. Out of the polar natures of consciousness, explained Vatsyana, there arose a difference in the consciousness of pleasure. The man would think, "This woman is united with me," while the woman would see it as "I am united with this man." According to this premise, the man's sexual consciousness is intrinsically one of conquest and possession and the woman's is one of yielding and surrender.

Vatsyayana's opinion, however, is not the whole truth, because within a man's nature there is also a passive and more feminine side, while within the woman there is a masculine and assertive aspect. While the masculine or feminine nature of either partner usually prevails according to their gender, a greater sense of wholeness in lovemaking is achieved when both sexes are allowed to express and act out their whole nature. Thus a man should be able to feel passive and yielding at times, just as the woman should feel free to be sexually assertive and expressive.

Compatible Unions

The *Kama Sutra* focuses its teachings on the arts of sensual pleasure so, quite rightly, it places a high value on sexual compatibility. This it defines with regard to three sexual factors: the dimensions of the sexual organs, the intensity of the passion, and the duration of an individual's lovemaking.

Comparative Dimensions

The original text is imaginatively descriptive about these matters. It categorizes men and women into classifications of animals, based on the dimensions of their genitals. Depending on whether a man's *lingam* is small, medium or large, he is known as a hare man, a bull man or a horse man. Likewise, according to the depth of a woman's *yoni*, she is known as a deer woman, a mare woman, or an elephant woman.

While a man and a woman each bring different but complementary qualities to their lovemaking, both should feel free to express the passive and assertive aspects of their sexual natures.

When a man makes love to a woman whose *yoni* is of a smaller depth than the length of his *lingam*, that intercourse is termed "high union"; if he makes love to a woman on the farthest end of the spectrum, such as coitus between the horse man and the deer woman, it is called "highest union." If a woman has sex with a man who is somewhat smaller in size than her it is called "low union," and, if for example, an elephant woman makes love to a hare man, it is called "lowest union." The *Kama Sutra* suggests that there are nine varieties of sexual union of equal and unequal dimensions and advises, unsurprisingly, that the equal union of a couple with similar dimensions is best. It then goes on to suggest that high union is better than low union, highest and lowest are the most unsatisfactory forms of copulation, and all other varieties are of middling degrees of sexual compatibility.

Sexual adjustments

The *Kama Sutra*'s discussion on genital dimensions is somewhat cold and analytical. It lacks reference to the emotional warmth which should exist between partners and which contributes greatly towards overcoming initial sexual difficulties. In reality, while genital sizes may play a role in sexual compatibility, unless there is a marked discrepancy between a man and a woman's genital dimensions, this is rarely a major factor in its attainment.

Sometimes a couple achieve complete sexual compatibility right from the start of their relationship. Anatomically, their body shapes and sizes are a perfect match, and without too much manoeuvering, their genital organs fit "like a glove." However, it is far more usual for real sexual compatibility to develop over a period of time. As lovers become familiar with one another's bodies, they adjust their pace, rhythms, movements and positions to suit one

another and so their lovemaking becomes naturally more harmonious.

Below are some of the sexual positions suggested by the *Kama Sutra* to assist compatibility in both high and low union.

Position for high union

A woman's vagina is about 3–4 inches (7–10cm) in length, and when it is in an unaroused state its walls are folded in against each other. However, when the woman is adequately sexually stimulated, the vaginal walls become engorged with blood fed from their plentiful supply of blood vessels. In a state of full arousal, the lower end of the vagina constricts while the internal upper portion swells out, thus creating the perfect receptacle to accommodate the man's penis. In addition, the vagina secretes its "love juices," exuding a special lubricant which facilities the penetration and thrusting of the penis.

Difficulties over penetration are most frequently a result of insufficient arousal rather than of genital dimensions. The woman may be sexually unaroused because of anxiety, stress, or inadequate foreplay, or because she is simply not turned on by her partner. When the woman is in the mood for sex, is relaxed and receptive, and has a skillful and tender lover who is both sensual and passionate, she should be able to receive her lover's *lingam* inside her *yoni* comfortably.

If the situation occurs that the male member is exceptionally large, or the woman's vagina is narrower and shorter than usual, care must be taken that penetration happens in a sensitive manner so as not to cause her pain. Most importantly, the man must

The 'widely opened position' adopted by the woman helps her partner to penetrate her more easily, especially if he is well endowed.

ensure that his partner is sufficiently aroused for the psychological and physiological reasons already explained. He must take care not to thrust into her before she is ready, and time should be given for her to adjust her positions for maximum comfort. The *Kama Sutra* suggests the following sexual positions for high union.

Widely opened position

Tilting your hips slightly upwards enables penetration to occur more easily, especially if your *yoni* is small or your lover's *lingam* is large. Lower your head and raise your pelvis upwards either by placing a pillow comfortably beneath your buttocks, or by pressing your feet against the mattress as a lever. Your thighs should open widely, exposing your vulva. Your lover can use his fingers to spread your love juices around the lips of your vagina and over the clitoris. If necessary, a small amount of water-soluble lubricant can be massaged on to these parts. He can also rub his *lingam* against your vulva for additional stimulation, giving you time to prepare sufficiently for penetration. Use your hand to guide his member into your *yoni* if necessary, remembering that too much haste at this delicate time can cause the *lingam* to slip out of the *yoni*. If this does happen, do not become embarrassed. Be playful with each other, and adjust your positions so that entry becomes possible.

The Rising Position

Once your lover has entered you, this position allows for deeper penetration. If you raise your legs up in the air on each side of your lover's body, your vagina is widened and your genital area is more exposed to your partner. He can increase your stimulation by rubbing his fingers gently against your clitoris. However, unless you are very fit, you will find this position too difficult to maintain for long.

The Yawning Position

This position is described more fully on page 126, but it is important to mention it here because it widens and lengthens your vagina, enabling deeper penetration. Your legs are still raised, but this time they rest against your partner's shoulders. He will be kneeling as he thrusts and he may clasp your legs protectively to his chest.

The Position of the Wife of Indra

Indra, the Hindu God of thunder and rain, and King of the Heavens, had a wife who was called Indrani, after whom this sexual posture is named. This position, says the *Kama Sutra*, is only learned with practice, but is recommended for "high union" to allow deeper penetration of the penis into a smaller vagina. It requires you to double your legs up on to the sides of your torso, so that your pelvis is tipped upwards. It probably can only be recommended if you are loosely jointed or well practiced in yoga. If you do try it, you won't want to stay too long in this posture. The man is definitely in control here, but you may find it exciting

to physically condense yourself in this way, containing and intensifying the sexual sensations.

The Superior Position

If you assume the Superior Position, which means you are sitting or kneeling on top of the man, you can control the depth of penetration more easily, in addition to the manner of the movements. The man should avoid thrusting unexpectedly so as to avoid banging painfully against your cervix.

A Matter of Size

Does the size of the man's penis affect his partner's sexual satisfaction? This is a question often dwelt upon by sex writers and by lovers themselves. It is a sensitive matter, for it goes straight to the heart of a man's delicate ego about his sexual prowess. Men are generally very concerned about penis sizes – an anxiety which begins in boyhood, when comparisons of penis shapes and sizes are made among peer groups in locker rooms and showers.

The standard answer to the question is usually that it does not matter, because it is the man that a woman loves, not his penis, and she draws her sexual happiness from making love with her chosen partner. Also, a penis which is small while flaccid can still compare favourably with that of a better endowed man once it is erect. In fact, in terms of female sexual satisfaction, the width of the penis is more important than its length. In addition, the size of the penis is not indicative of

*A woman should adopt 'the rising position' if she
wants her partner to penetrate her deeply.*

the degree of a man's libido or virility – although it may affect his sexual confidence.

However, while all these facts are true, the readiness with which these reassurances are usually given often conceals a hurried attempt to protect the fragile male ego. Size can matter in some circumstances. A woman usually wants to "feel" her man inside her and if she does not have that sense of being filled by his *lingam* she may be secretly dissatisfied.

Low union

The problem may not be a matter of penis size; it could also be that the woman's vagina is wide or slack. This may be because of natural physiology, or a result of childbirth. When the dimensions are in such contrast it is wise to understand how certain positions can shorten or narrow the *yoni* so that it snugly contains the *lingam*. The supine and sideways Clasping and Pressing positions (see pages 123–4) are easy and intimate examples of how to achieve this purpose. Also, the woman can tighten her thighs together, or contract her vaginal muscles, to surround and clasp the penis more securely. The *Kama Sutra* calls this the Mare's position, describing it as when a woman "forcibly holds the *lingam* inside her *yoni*".

The Pressed Position

This more adventurous position for "low union" is described in the *Kama Sutra*. Here you draw your knees up to your chest and place your feet on your lover's chest as he kneels before you. This position will make your vagina more shallow and so happily accommodating for a penis of smaller length, but it requires suppleness in your limbs and hips and may be difficult to maintain for a long period. Also, the separation of your bodies may make you long for a more intimate cuddle. However, the comforting contact between your feet and his chest can more than compensate for this and it also feels good to involve the extremities of your body in the physical contact of lovemaking.

Orgasm before intercourse

In the situation where the man's erect penis is still too small to fully satisfy his partner during the coitus phase of lovemaking, the couple can still achieve sexual satisfaction if the man sufficiently arouses his partner before he penetrates her. The *Kama Sutra*, in its own inimitable style, advises: "If a man cannot satisfy a Hastini woman (elephant woman) he should use other means to excite her passion, and he should not have intercourse until she has become excited or experiences pleasure." In other words, the text suggests that by skillful and attentive foreplay, through caresses and kisses, and also, if desired, through manual stimulation and oral sex, the man can bring his partner to orgasm before he enters her.

The 'pressed position' is recommended by the Kama Sutra *for 'low union' – when a woman makes love to a man of smaller proportions.*

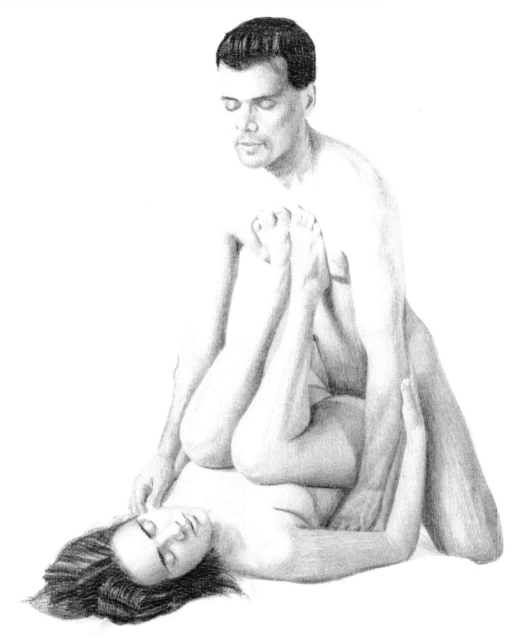

Force of passion

The *Kama Sutra* says that in both men and women alike there are three degrees of passion, which it calls small, middling, and intense. Clearly, a sexual relationship is at its most equitable when two lovers share a mutual level of desire.

There is no prescribed degree of libido which is right or wrong; each person has their own unique sexual rhythms and needs. Matching them to fit with another person is the secret to compatibility. For example, a warm, affectionate, and passionate woman would be unhappy if her partner was cold and unresponsive to her advances. Conversely, a woman whose sexual desire is moderate or low would feel pressurized if she felt that unrealistic sexual demands were being made upon her.

When there is a marked discrepancy in the force of sexual desire, the situation can easily lead to feelings of resentment or rejection. It requires great sensitivity and clear communication on behalf of both people to resolve their sexual differences so that a compatible sex life can be established.

When libido ebbs

Passion is usually at its strongest in the early stages of a relationship, and it is inevitable that over time the initial intensity of sexual desire will moderate itself as other areas of the relationship develop. A couple who can adjust to those changes, and yet still remain sexually satisfied, possess a vital key to relationship happiness.

If loss of libido is affecting you or your partner, it is important to look at the reasons why. Certain factors, such as poor health, tiredness, depression, caring for small children, stress at work, bereavement, and periods of low self-esteem, can all have a detrimental results on the libido. Unresolved tensions between the two of you can also adversely affect your sexual relationship.

You should neither isolate the problem as being the other person's fault, nor be too defensive to discuss or confront the issues for yourself. When a relationship of value passes through a period of sexual incompatibility and low libido, it is worth the effort to discover why and to find ways of restoring it to your mutual satisfaction.

Talk to each other about your sexual needs with sensitivity and tact, and listen openly to what the other has to say. Avoid blame, demand and criticism, all of which will be counter-productive. Seek a doctor's advice if either of you suspect that the lack of interest in sex is linked to a medical cause. Find ways to relax if your lifestyle has become hectic and stressful. Get out of the home for a dinner date or a long walk together, especially if this is the only opportunity you have to be alone together. Take short breaks, or a long holiday, and rediscover the fun-loving and spontaneous side of your relationship. Change your routines so you disrupt the comfortable monotony and humdrum of everyday existence that so often sounds the death knell to an active sex life. Laugh and cry together, and show your feelings so that you both remain emotionally alive and responsive to one another. Remain physically affectionate with each other even if the sex-drive has dipped.

Cuddle and massage each other to ensure that sensuality and intimacy between you continues to thrive. Try making love in unusual places and at unusual times, creating and acting out new and inspiring scenarios. A man and woman who determine to keep their communication and sexual life healthy and harmonious are building a strong foundation for the future of their relationship.

Saying no

Women are deeply conditioned to please men sexually and a woman may sometimes find herself engaging in sexual activity with her partner even when she is not in the mood to make love. Unlike a man, a woman can allow intercourse to happen even if she is not sexually aroused and is not fully participating.

In some circumstances, it is genuinely possible for a woman to gain a certain kind of pleasure from acquiescing to her partner's sexual needs even though she herself would not have initiated the event. However, it is very important for a woman to always feel she has autonomy over her own body and to know how to say "no" to sex when she does not want it.

For centuries, the institution of marriage in many cultures gave the man the right of ownership over his wife's body. Countless women have endured sexual relationships dictated by the whims and demands of their male partners with little consideration of their own desires and wishes. Every woman should have control over her own sexuality, with the fundamental right to refuse sex and to expect to be made love to in a respectful manner which is considerate of her own desires. Sometimes men misread the signals that women are giving in regard to their willingness for sex. When you are dating someone, be very clear about your sexual boundaries. Try not to become

The Kama Sutra *urges men to be sensitive to the needs and tender nature of women.*

61

involved in ambiguous situations which can lead to confusion. Until you know and trust the other person, it is better to avoid intimate scenarios which might be misinterpreted. For example, you may invite your date into your home for a late-night cup of coffee and mean just that, but you need to be sure that your invitation is not perceived as a code for a hidden agenda. While you have a right to expect that a man will be sensitive and respectful to you, staying in charge of your sexuality means taking responsibility for it at all times.

> " If a male be long-timed, the female loves him the more, but if he be short-timed she is dissatisfied with him. "

Timing

The ancient sexual teachings of the East, such as those found in the *Kama Sutra* and Tantric and Taoist texts, placed great importance on female pleasure and satisfaction in lovemaking. The sages of these cultures understood well a woman's sexual needs and orgasmic potential. A student of the arts of love learnt that an accomplished lover was one who knew how to please a woman by combining tenderness with skill; who took time to arouse her sufficiently and knew which sexual positions increased her delight. He also learnt how to temper his own passion to give the woman time to reach her own sexual fulfillment.

With regard to the duration of sexual intercourse, the *Kama Sutra* says that there are three kinds of men and women: the short-timed, the moderate-timed and the long-timed. It emphasizes, however, that a woman prefers the lover who is able to prolong foreplay and lovemaking, because female passion is slower to arouse but once ignited will last for a long time.

Clearly, the *Kama Sutra* is referring here to the orgasmic cycle of men and women. It recognizes that a woman may not reach an orgasm if her lover fails to arouse her sufficiently in foreplay, or if he ejaculates too quickly. It points out that once a man has ejaculated his desire is likely to fade, while a woman's desire may actually increase after reaching her climax.

Orgasmic compatibility

In a sexually harmonious relationship the attainment of orgasm should be a mutually satisfying experience. Orgasm for both sexes can be intensely pleasurable and it is perceived by most couples as the pinnacle of their lovemaking.

The greater sexual openness of the last decades has enabled women to become more confident about their sexuality and orgasmic potential. Most modern women expect to have their sexual needs met, and to be made love to in such a way that they too can achieve the fulfillment of orgasm. The

The desire to please your partner on an emotional and sexual level, in addition to satisfying oneself, will create a precious bond between lovers.

majority of men are also more aware of female sexuality, and it has become important to them to try to satisfy their partners in lovemaking.

Clitoral stimulation

Most women need to receive sustained clitoral stimulation to achieve an orgasm, and certain sexual positions are particularly advantageous in this regard (see pages 123–8). The man can also arouse his partner by tender manual or oral stimulation of her clitoris, but he should do this sensitively and as part of a total approach to lovemaking. It can be irritating and uncomfortable for a woman to have attention focused solely and directly on her clitoris, or to have her lover rub it monotonously in an attempt to arouse her to orgasm. In particular, the woman should be already aroused by loving foreplay, and producing some vaginal lubrication before active contact with the clitoris is made. Teach your lover how he should touch and kiss you in such an intimate place.

It is not at all unusual for some women to have difficulties in reaching a vaginal orgasm during intercourse, though in every other respect their sexual responses are perfectly normal. If this is true for you, and if you desire it, your lover can orally or manually stimulate you to a clitoral orgasm before he enters you or after his own ejaculation.

> **"Auddalika says: Males, when engaged in coition, cease of themselves after emission, and are satisfied, but it is not so with females."**

The multiorgasmic woman

Unlike their male partners, a number of women are multiorgasmic and are able to experience a series of climaxes during one session of lovemaking. The opposite quote from the *Kama Sutra* illustrates that the sages of old were well aware of this fact. The "fall of semen", in this context, is evidently a term for orgasm.

In the book *Heterosexuality*, the eminent sex researchers Masters and Johnson state that all women have the capacity to be multiorgasmic although most are not. Their view is that women are more likely to be multiorgasmic as a result of self-masturbation or oral sex, rather than during intercourse, and this implies that direct clitoral stimulation is a major factor in creating the multiorgasmic response.

A multiorgasmic woman may seem a threatening prospect for a man who is not confident about his own sexuality. He may feel that he can never hope to satisfy his mate and that he will be overwhelmed by her libido. It is even possible that a woman will subdue her sexuality out of fear of intimidating her partner. A woman who has an expansive and ecstatic sexuality should seek a partner who celebrates her erotic prowess and is able to prolong his lovemaking so that she can be completely fulfilled.

No pressure

The attainment of orgasm is only one aspect of lovemaking, and it should never become the single dominating factor. The psychological pressure on women to reach an orgasm during intercourse, and the performance-related anxiety men experience in trying to please their partners sexually can be counter-productive to compatible lovemaking.

Do not allow yourself to feel pressured into having an orgasm. If your lover is working overtime doing all the "right" things to you, and it is making you feel exhausted or obliged to produce a result, then ask him to slow down. Come back to the moment, hold each other, breathe together, and allow your lovemaking to regain its spontaneity. Many women can be sexually fulfilled by the physical and emotional intimacy of sexual intercourse without feeling it necessary to climax every time they make love.

The orgasmic cycle

The research done in the 1950s by Masters and Johnson confirmed what the ancient teaching had always stated – that the arousal and orgasmic cycle follows a similar pattern in men and women, though there are some differences in the duration of each of its phases. The research showed that there are four stages of sexual response for both genders. Understanding the male and female patterns of response can help you to become more sexually compatible.

> **"** The fall of the semen of the man takes place only at the end of coition, while the semen of the woman falls continually; and after the semen of both has all fallen away, then they wish for the discontinuance of coition. **"**

The arousal phase

This first phase usually involves anticipation, foreplay, and the early stages of intercourse, during which period you and your lover become sexually excited. Generally, visual stimulation is a strong factor for men, whereas touching and caressing is more likely to ignite your passion. Your man may become excited quicker than you, but if he is a sensitive lover he will enjoy arousing you fully with caresses and kisses over your whole body.

As the mutual excitement intensifies, you may both experience similar physiological changes such as an increase in neuro-muscular tension and in heart rate and blood pressure, and in both sexes the nipples may become erect. Your female arousal response will cause your vulva lips and clitoris to swell, and your vagina to expand at its upper end. Your vaginal walls will begin to secrete a sexual lubrication. Meanwhile, the increased blood flow in your partner's penis will cause it to become erect.

The plateau phase

This is the coitus period of lovemaking, during which you have progressed from foreplay to intercourse and the thrusting motions of sexual activity are taking place. During this stage, you and your partner should try to synchronize your rhythm so that you can change gracefully from one position to another and continue to stay harmoniously attuned to each other. During the plateau phase, your arousal state will probably maintain a fairly high but steady pitch. At times the level of intensity may become subdued as your embraces are focused on emotional intimacy rather than physical excitement, or it may increase as you regain the excitement and stimulation of more erotically charged activity. These changes may cause the vaginal lubrications to fluctuate in quantity as you pass through a variety of sexual moods.

As the woman, you will probably find it easier than your partner to sustain this plateau phase. You partner should try to moderate his arousal levels so that he does not reach the point of ejaculation inevitability prematurely or before you are quite ready to climax. You can help by not overstimulating him with your pelvic movements. Work out familiar signals to alert each other when either of you need to slow down to regain your equilibrium.

The plateau phase of sexual union is the time when both partners can relax into their lovemaking and take delight in each other's bodies.

During the plateau phase, and particularly as you approach an orgasm, certain physiological changes are taking place for both of you. Your breathing may become more shallow and rapid as your hearts pump faster. Both sexes may experience a reddish flush spreading across the chest and neck.

Your female sexual response may cause your breasts to swell slightly and enlarge the dark-pigmented areola which surrounds your nipples. Your vagina continues to expand and lengthen, your uterus elevates, your clitoris retracts into its hood, and the lips of your vulva become increasingly swollen and dark in colour.

Your partner's male sexual response will cause his penis to harden, and its head to enlarge slightly from increased blood flow. His testes will elevate closer towards his body and at this stage, he may begin to emit some pre-ejaculatory fluid.

Orgasm

Orgasm is the highly pleasurable release of tension which has built up within your bodies as a result of sexual stimulation. You will experience it as a series of strong, involuntary rhythmic contractions emanating from your genital and pelvic area, and possibly spreading over your whole body in wave-like sensations.

It is important for you to understand what is happening to your man at these moments of his climax. Just prior to his orgasm and ejaculation, he will experience rhythmic contractions originating from the area of his prostate gland. Once

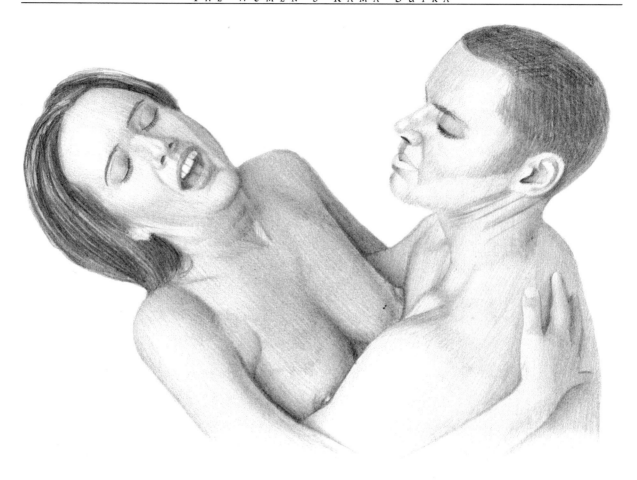

Both sexes share a similar response to sexual orgasm, experiencing it as a pulsating wave of intensely pleasurable sensations.

these have begun he no longer has control over his orgasm, and this event is known as the moment of "ejaculatory inevitability." This is followed by another series of powerful contractions emanating from the base of his penis which propels the semen out at the top. These contractions and the pumping sensation which follows are extremely pleasurable for him.

Your experience of orgasm is not so different in essence from your lover's. Once you have reached your sexual peak, provided you do not lose the correct type of stimulation or your own concentration, there will begin a series of powerful rhythmic muscular contractions in the region of your pelvis and genital area. The sensation of these contractions can feel like a series of mild and delightful pulsations, or may be so strong that your whole body feels as though powerful waves of energy are sweeping through it. During this time of release you may gasp, cry or even scream out with emotion. Temporarily, your facial muscles, hands or feet may spasm, and some women describe the experience as a "little death," or something akin to a momentary loss of consciousness. The more you are able to surrender your body to these waves of releasing energy, the greater your ogasmic joy will be.

Resolution

After making love and attaining orgasm, your bodies will return naturally to their non-aroused state. This is the perfect time to lie quietly together in each other's arms, and to continue the intimacy of your lovemaking in a quiet and harmonious manner. For your man, this is a necessary period of rest and for some time it will be physically impossible for him to regain a full erection or to ejaculate again. How long is dependent on individual factors, such as his age and general vigour, or even on how much sexual activity he has had in the previous days. The younger the

man, the quicker he may be able to engage again in sexual intercourse. However, there is no reason why affectionate contact cannot be maintained between you both and probably, like most women, you place a high value on these particular moments of closeness.

If you are highly aroused but did not attain orgasm, you may feel restless and uncomfortable during his resolution period because the vaso-congestion in your pelvic area has not yet returned to normal, leaving you feeling sexually dissatisfied. You may still want to reach an orgasm, and if your lover is attentive to your needs he can continue to stimulate you orally and manually. He can suck and kiss your breasts and nipples and gently rub or lick your clitoris, so bringing you to your climax.

Seeking help

Sexual incompatibility can seriously undermine the strongest of relationships, and even with the best will in the world it is not always possible for the partners involved to resolve the problems on their own. In a relationship that is basically committed and loving it is important that the man and woman remain supportive of one another and open to honest communication about their sexual difficulties. Blaming one another will only lessen the chance of overcoming their sexual problems because the very nature of an enduring and satisfying sexual relationship is based on trust, respect, and love.

Psychosexual issues

Psychosexual problems, which are not medically based, often have their roots in anxieties or unconscious fears which originate from childhood or adolescence. Also, as couples settle down, have families and mature, many new issues affecting their libido may arise. Most sexual dysfunctions can be successfully treated with the help of a trained and sympathetic psychosexual counsellor. There is no more shame or failure in seeking expert professional help in sexual matters than in seeking medical advice for an illness.

Psychosexual treatment may begin by encouraging the couple to initially liberate themselves from the psychological stress which occurs around the pressure of having to achieve successful sexual intercourse. Instead, it may encourage them to go back to the essential basics of sensual physical

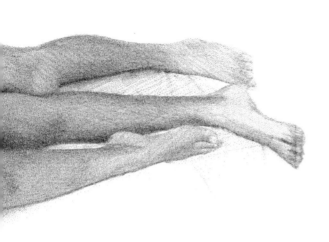

Even if he has ejaculated before she is completely sexually satisfied, a loving man can continue to stimulate his partner towards orgasm.

where the couple refamiliarize themselves with each other's bodies without the burden of performance-related anxiety, and where they explore their issues around the giving and receiving of attention. These exercises, known as Sensate Focus, were originally developed by the sex researchers Masters and Johnson, and are widely used in sex therapy to help couples overcome many sexual dysfunctions. Problems which affect men, such as impotency, premature or retarded ejaculation, and fear of intimacy, can be resolved with sensitive sex therapy. Likewise, the treatment of female sexual dysfunctions such as sexual disinterest, inability to attain orgasm, and fear of penetration have a high success rate. Vaginismus, a distressing female psychosomatic disorder where the fear of penetration causes a spasm of the muscles at the entrance of the vagina, has a very positive prognosis when treated properly by responsible psychosexual therapy.

Gaining a perspective

Some of the conditions mentioned above can be self-treated by following certain therapeutic exercises. However, the guidance of a sex counsellor is important because their objective and sensitive intervention enables either or both partners to gain a better perspective about their personal problems, and to assist them to overcome their fears, resistances and potential areas of relationship strife.

contact, where over a period of time, and in a progression of exercises, the couple forgo sexual and genital stimulation in order to rediscover the wonder and pleasures of affectionate touching and massage. In a sense it is like a new beginning,

CHAPTER THREE

Astrological Compatibility

"The sun, moon, stars and planets,
and other heavenly bodies
appear to work intentionally
for the good of the world."

Astrology is an ancient science that has been used in India for thousands of years. It is difficult to know just how old it is because much of the Vedic tradition was transmitted orally, and was preserved by being passed on from one generation to the next. However, it is clear that for thousands of years, the Indian Tantric masters and disciples closely adhered to the science of astrology for spiritual, philosophical and practical purposes.

In the land from which the *Kama Sutra* originated, astrology has been used traditionally to foretell the future of individuals, kingdoms and even wars. In particular, it has been instrumental in the selection of suitable partners for marriage. Indian custom is that marriages are arranged by the parents or other family of the bride and groom. Among other factors, the parents will consult the astrological chart of the prospective partner of their offspring in order to determine his or her suitability and how compatible the pair will be. A potential bride's birth chart will be examined by the groom's family to ascertain her qualities as a wife, and to ensure that she is of a virtuous and loyal nature. Her health and success at childbearing will be another important consideration.

In India, tradition holds that marriage is an unbreakable spiritual and practical commitment for life, and love will grow and mature from this solid foundation. Arranged marriages have generally proved to be successful even though it is often the case that the man and woman have not been alone, or have not even met, before their wedding day.

For Western couples, however, arranged marriages are a thing of the past. Nowadays, people generally select their partners on the basis of sexual attraction and overt compatibility. On the whole, marriages and partnerships are entered into freely, and the role of astrology, if it is used at all, is either to help us to understand our relationship, or simply to provide us with entertainment.

Birth charts

Most of you will be familiar with some of the basic concepts of astrology and you probably know your Sun sign – for example, whether you are a Libran or a Taurean. However, if you choose to delve more deeply into astrology and its influence on your choice of partners, you will need to have your birth chart drawn up. For this, you will require the help of an astrologer. The chart has to be very precise, and your exact time of birth is essential to its accuracy. You will soon discover that astrology is a much more complex issue than the horoscopes that appear in the popular press would suggest. Other planets have an effect on your chart and influence you – for example, the Moon governs your emotions. Your chart is also divided into 12 houses which refer to specific aspects of your life, such as work or love, and the planets which rule those houses have a direct influence upon the particular areas they represent. When looking for an astrologically compatible relationship, you would want to consult those planets which influence your Seventh House, which is also known as the House of Love, and is ruled by Venus and Libra. An astrologer will look at the Seventh House in your birth chart to determine your attitude to one-to-one relationships. Any planets that are placed in this house will have a powerful effect on your attitude to commitment and relationship. In addition, the star sign on the cusp (at the beginning) of the Seventh House is another important factor in revealing your attitudes towards love.

The subject of astrology is covered in much more detail in other books, but it is interesting to look at some of the key astrological determinants which help you to clarify your requirements and assess your compatibility when you are seeking a potential mate. Obviously, many other things can determine compatibility, so astrology should be considered as part of a larger picture.

The Sun signs

Your Sun is usually your dominant aspect and will reflect your fundamental qualities and identity. It is probably the basic force that motivates you and it will highlight your strongest character attributes and expectations of life. Other planets in your natal chart may have an effect on your Sun sign, and this will explain why you possess some of the characteristics of another sign.

Illustration of the Taurus sign in a 16th-century Turkish treatise on astrology. Taureans are sensual but earthy people. A woman born under this sign may seek a secure relationship and will enjoy the arts of home-making.

Aries

This is the first sign of the horoscope. Arians are usually forceful, confident and self-assertive people who are direct in their actions and inclined to be competitive. If you are born under this Fire sign you may be good at initiating action, such as providing the stimulus for a new love affair. However, you might find it difficult to sustain your initial enthusiasm. You can be quite self-absorbed, and are therefore likely to put your own needs before your partner's.

An Aries woman is usually strong in spirit and is therefore drawn to a rugged and masculine man. A man born under another Fire sign will appeal to you. You could become involved with a Sagittarian because of his sense of adventure or a Leo man because of his unequivocal maleness and his aura of glamour. However, the fieriness of this combination will cause the sparks to fly, as you are unlikely to be the compliant female that he seeks.

Taurus

Women born under the sign of Taurus, the first Earth sign of the Zodiac, are usually very sensual and take delight in the pleasures of the earth. As a Taurean, you are probably reliable and productive but possibly a little stubborn and reluctant to change. You will look for security in your relationships but you will enter a commitment cautiously, and only when most of your needs are met, not just your sexual ones. However, you will take your com-

mitment seriously, and may even become possessive of your partner. You are a good homemaker, and you will probably fill your house with beautiful items.

As a Taurean woman, you will look for men who also possess earthy qualities. You could find contentment with a Capricorn or Virgo who will share your appreciation of fine things and homemaking. You might, however, be swept off your feet by a Leo male, who in the early stages of courtship will wine and dine you. However, you could become disenchanted with your Leo friend, who will fail to share your enthusiasm for day-to-day concerns.

Gemini

Gemini is an Air sign, and if you are born under this sign you are probably a great communicator with a wide variety of friends. You are preoccupied with acquiring facts and have an interest in many things. However, you find it difficult to sustain your interest in any one particular area, and this trait may appear fickle and superficial to others. A Gemini has difficulty with commitment, always believing that someone better is just around the corner. You are likely to settle down a little later in life than most other signs. At times, your partner may find you emotionally detached and remote. However, he will be delighted by your quick mind, charm and wit.

You will be attracted to men who have unusual careers and personalities. Geminis and Sagittarians are often drawn to each other, although they are on the opposite sides of the Zodiac. The flamboyant Leo may appeal to you but he might feel threatened by all your diverse interests. Opposites can attract, and a liason with a Capricorn is an unlikely match which could work if your very different personalities complement each other. He can provide the stability you yearn for, and you will definitely keep him entertained. The critical mind of the Virgo will upset you and a relationship with this Earth sign may not prove to be a long-lasting match.

Cancer

If you are born under the sign of the crab you are most probably a sensitive, caring person, with a very nurturing and feminine nature. However, you may be unnecessarily cautious with people as you do not want to be hurt. Moodiness can hamper your relationships and inhibit your vitality. You flourish in a secure and loving relationship and will be devoted to your family.

As a gentle person, you may appreciate the strong, capable qualities of a Taurean man. His more traditional values will probably complement your need for home and family. You may be excited by the free-spirited Sagittarian man, but he is unlikely to provide you with the stability that you crave. Happiness can be found with the gentle Piscean who will understand your moods and probable timidity. While a Cancerian man may initially feel like a kindred spirit, and therefore an ideal match, you may discover that the relationship lacks dynamism.

Leo

You are a loyal, warm and radiant woman. You are probably very creative and if this aspect is unfulfilled you can become very unhappy. As a Leo, you have fiery emotions and you love to be in love, so you have a tendency to put your chosen partner on a pedestal, making him feel special and adored. However, you expect your loyalty to be returned in equal measure, and if your partner does not share every aspect of your life, you can easily feel betrayed. As a true romantic, you want to be admired by your mate. You will appreciate someone who lavishes attention on you, and gifts of flowers and jewellery will be much appreciated by you. You need a man who will cherish you, and a strong Aries could be a good match because his ardent emotions will match your own. The interesting mind of an Aquarian may initially attract you, but his coolness and detachment could hurt you and therefore the match may not endure.

Virgo

You are likely to be a perfectionist, and because you have a tendency to be analytical and discriminating, others may perceive you as critical. Virgo is not a particularly emotional sign and you may be uncomfortable expressing your feelings or even dealing with your partner's emotions. You want to be the perfect mate, although this is inevitably an impossible goal for anyone to achieve. You prefer men who are not given to excesses of emotion, so you will probably be

incompatible with the fiery Aries and Leo man. You could find a meeting of minds with the intellectual Aquarian man, while your idealized concept of love could find resonance with a Libran. Virgos and Scorpios can make an interesting alliance, provided you can handle the latter's secretive and deeply emotional nature. However, the depth of the Scorpio's feelings may act as a perfect complement to your tendency for coolness.

Libra

Your Sun is ruled by the planet Venus, so you are born to love. Libran women are sociable and graceful, with a gift for relating to others. You have a strong sense of fairness and justice, but your desire to please others may mean that you are not always direct or truthful.

When in love, you know how to fulfill your partner's desire. You are attracted to partners whose lifestyles you admire and who are strong and decisive. Therefore, the charismatic Aries would complement your personality but you would want him to share your love for the arts and music. The complex emotional nature of a Cancerian could prove difficult, and although you might be initially attracted to the adventurous Sagittarian, his bluntness could have a cooling effect on your affection.

The Leo woman emanates the radiance of her Sun sign, but she demands loyalty and passion in return for her devotion. Illustration from a 16th-century Turkish treatise on astrology.

Scorpio

Scorpios have a reputation for being the most sexual sign of the Zodiac. They possess intense emotions and are very intuitive. As a Scorpio woman, you probably have strong physical and emotional resources, and you seek deep and merging sexual relationships. The depth of your feelings makes you vulnerable, but you are secretive about your emotions. However, if you do not express yourself, and use your energy, you can easily become jealous and restless.

You could find yourself attracted to a Sagittarian because you share a depth of character, but the relationship could contain conflict because of your secretive nature and the Sagittarian need to state the facts. Your soulmate may be a Cancerian, who, like you, shares a yearning for profound emotional exchange. You could also find a lasting connection with a Piscean, who also desires a merging of souls with his beloved. Scorpios, probably more than any other sign of the Zodiac, can find lasting relationships with those born under the same sign.

Sagittarius

You are enthusiastic and optimistic, with a philosophical outlook on life. You value mental and physical freedom, and you hate to feel tied down or trapped. You enjoy a variety of interests and you want to be constantly stimulated intellectually. You are an idealistic person who will give your partner what you want for yourself, which is a sense of freedom.

The fun-loving and mentally stimulating Gemini will be attractive to you. Your forthright manner and verbal directness may scare off the gentle Piscean or the sensitive Cancerian. You will be drawn to the charismatic Leo but you might find yourself in competition with him, and you certainly will not want to be dominated. Aries, your fellow Fire sign, could prove a successful match since you both share a love of adventure. The possessiveness of Taureans or Scorpios will be a major deterrent for the Sagittarian woman, who does not want to be accountable to anyone.

Capricorn

A Capricorn woman is usually self-controlled, traditional, and ambitious, and values hard work. She can make an excellent partner, capable of contributing to the relationship in many practical ways. However, conflict could occur because she may sometimes put her work before spending time with her man or family.

As a Capricorn, you know how to enjoy yourself without losing sight of your goals. You will seek a strong and dependable partner, and the Taurean or Virgo man could share your enthusiasm for working and building something together. Your somewhat taciturn demeanour may clash with the more frivolous aspects of a capricious Gemini, and the Leo's overt display of emotion may leave you unimpressed.

Aquarius

You are an individualist with an urge for freedom.

Others may see you as eccentric, but you are tolerant and friendly to other people. In an intimate situation, however, your partner may feel that you are emotionally detached. You are an idealist, and this can prove a difficulty in enduring relationships, because an idealized state is not always possible. With Aquarians, mere physical charm is not enough, and you will also seek a partner whose intelligence you admire and with whom you can indulge in witty and idealistic discussions. However, you have a need for fun and laughter, and so you may find yourself compatible with a fun-loving but mentally stimulating Gemini. You could have an affinity with Librans, and the Virgo trait to view love as an idealized state is in tune with your own ideas, but the relationship could lack warmth of emotion. The enthusiasm and passionate views of a Sagittarian are likely to enthral you.

Pisces

As a compassionate Piscean, you have the capacity to empathize with others. In a relationship, this gift can sometimes cause you to over-identify with your partner and neglect your own needs. You are a true romantic, appreciating gifts and love notes, and you easily fall in love.

You like to nurture your partner but you also love to be cuddled and held. A Cancerian partner could offer you the tenderness that you long for. The decisive personalities of Leos and Aries men may attract you, but their lack of patience could fail to take your sensitivity into consideration.

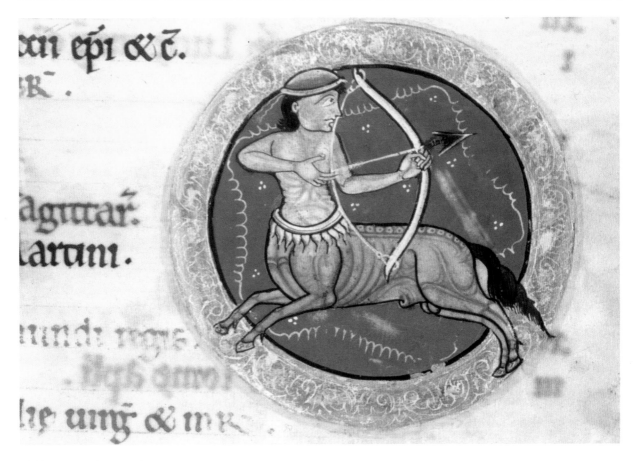

Mars and Venus: love and desire

The planets Mars and Venus exert a strong influence on the realms of love, sex and relationships. Mars is perceived as the male principle of love and affects your sexual energy. For a woman, it may represent a strong ideal of the kind of man she is attracted to; for example, if you have Mars in Taurus in your natal chart, you may be attracted to strong, earthy types of men. For a man, it can rep-

Illustration from an English Psalter, York c. 1170. The Sagittarian woman values her freedom and is very idealistic. She will want a partner who respects her freedom.

resent the way in which he asserts himself in his sexual behaviour.

Venus is the love principle in a chart. It symbol-

izes love, affection, and sensual pleasures. Venus will show the way that you express affection and the kind of experiences you need to feel loved by someone, as well as indicating the female qualities and the types of activities that you need to develop in order to feel feminine and desirable. For example, if you have Venus in Taurus, you are likely to be a very sensual person, and have a particular enjoyment of expensive and luxurious beauty care. If your Venus is in Cancer, then you will need to find a partner who will truly appreciate your loving, caring and nurturing nature. Venus in a man's chart may show the type of woman he finds sexually attractive, and it will indicate his ideals in love and relationships.

Any aspects between Mars in one person's chart with Venus in the other person's could show that there is a strong physical attraction between the two people.

The planets Venus and Mars, personified here on canvas by Botticelli, represent the female and male principles of love and sex.

Synastry

If you are curious about your compatibility with someone and you have an interest in astrology, you may want to explore the whole issue a little more deeply. For this you will need to seek the advice of an astrologer for a synastry reading. Synastry is the comparison of two people's birth charts and it will reveal their compatibility.

In synastry, the charts are compared and any strong aspects are explored – harmonious aspects as well as more problematic ones. Usually, if there is a strong connection between two people, there will be complementary and opposite aspects between their charts. Harmonious aspects mean that there is the potential for compatibility in an area of the relationship. An opposition between the two charts could indicate an area of tension which may lead to misunderstandings and conflicts. A conflict, however, is not always a negative influence – it can also create a certain dynamism and vitality in the relationship. Understanding these astrological tensions can help you to appreciate your differences and, in turn, strengthen your relationship.

CHAPTER FOUR

The Importance of Physical Affection

> " Women being of a tender nature,
> want tender beginnings. "

Physical affection is an essential aspect of any relationship and couples should endeavour to ensure that it remains an integral part of their intimate communication, not only as an expression of their sexual attraction to each other but also as a means of fostering an ongoing sense of intimacy, appreciation and caring. Truly sensual lovers are those who delight in all the subtle nuances of tactile contact, from handholding and loving cuddles to sensual foreplay and lovemaking. A couple who can respond physically and emotionally to one another through the right kind of embrace, a sensitive touch, or a caring massage have the key to nurturing their relationship through both the good and the difficult times.

The *Kama Sutra* devotes a lot of its teaching to the importance of sensual, tactile contact between a man and woman. While it focuses specifically on the art of sensitive and creative foreplay as a prelude to sexual happiness, the sages of that era also knew that emotional contentment was derived from the continued sharing of physical affection throughout all areas of the relationship.

Tactile sensuality

Women are generally far more in tune with the need for continuing sensuality within a relationship than are men. They know that a successful sexual relationship cannot survive indefinitely without the nurturing input of a spontaneous and loving touch which exists for its own sake, rather than purely as a prelude to sexual intercourse.

It is not uncommon for women to complain that they feel deprived of tactile sensuality once their relationship has become established. They miss the romantic moments of holding hands, of caring cuddles, of longlasting kisses and melting embraces that characterized the initial stages of their relationship. For the woman, these loving gestures may be more emotionally satisfying than sexual intercourse. They are an affirmation of continuing affection and regard between her and her lover, and they maintain her confidence in the security and intimacy of their partnership.

Men, of course, equally appreciate a physically warm relationship, though some may attach less importance to romantic tactile gestures than their female partners. What came naturally to a man in the early stages of wooing may seem superfluous in the circumstances of an established relationship. He may feel that the real value of his commitment to his partner is demonstrated by his continued involvement in the relationship and his practical contribution to it, and may fail to grasp the real significance his partner places on his physical attentiveness. He delivers a perfunctory peck on the cheek, and she longs for a lingering kiss. He gives her a quick hug, and she would prefer a warm embrace. Sex itself may become more functional, bypassing the long, luxurious foreplay of earlier

---

In his painting The Birth of Venus *Botticelli exalts in his art the sensual form and nature of women. The painting depicts Venus, the goddess of love, rising from the ocean.*

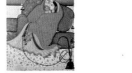

times, hastening instead towards penetration and release without the sweetness of those earlier caring caresses. Sensuality can be a casualty of familiarity, but couples ignore it at their risk because boredom and indifference can fill the space that is left by its departure.

Physical affection is, in a strange way, a more significant expression of intimacy and closeness than the actual act of sexual intercourse. While intercourse can be performed in response to a sexual urge, out of duty, or almost as if on automatic pilot, sensual touching arises out of genuinely tender feelings and is hard to fake. For example, it is well known that many women working as prostitutes refuse to let their customers kiss their mouths, regarding that as too personal a physical exchange.

Keeping sensuality alive

Once the spontaneous physical warmth has died in a relationship it is hard to revive it. It is better never to let the flame of physical affection die out, and both partners should be alert to the conditions that can diminish it. For example, try not to take each other for granted, even if your partnership is firmly established. Always remind yourself of the qualities in your partner that made you love and appreciate him in the first place. Respect each other's differing opinions, and give each other the freedom to be individuals.

Talk through issues that are bothering you before they cause tension between you, because once either of you becomes resentful, it is harder to be communicative and spontaneously affectionate. The withdrawal of physical affection is sometimes a subtle method of getting revenge.

Making an effort

Continue to make the effort to stay attractive to your partner and, not least, do it also for your own self-esteem. Do not slip into sloppy routines or forgo the care of your personal hygiene. While there is a certain relief in being able to relax and be comfortable with your partner, familiarity is no excuse for letting yourself go. This does not mean, however, that you are expected to remain some kind of Barbie doll to keep your man's attention, or that you should be afraid of letting your growing maturity show itself proudly in your appearance. The careful attention you pay to your health, fitness and appearance at any stage of your life will send the right signals to your partner, and he will feel complimented by your efforts. Of course, you can expect the same input from your partner, and praising him on his appearance and affirming his manliness will encourage him to remain attractive and attentive to you.

Be constructive

Affection is the first casualty of an onslaught of criticism, nagging and undermining. None of these are effective forms of communication and indeed they are guaranteed to drive the recipient into a "bunker mentality" from which sensual affection is bound to wither. Learn to be creative in your communication. Say what you need to say directly rather than in an attacking or manipulative way, and learn to differentiate between essential and minor issues before you blow trivial matters out of all proportion.

Constant attention

A sensual and affectionate relationship is one that needs constant care and attention. It needs to be nurtured with love and respect. The physical communication between you and your partner should always remain alive and active outside the bedroom, expressing itself in a multitude of tactile gestures. Foster sensuality in your lovemaking too, extending your foreplay into a luxurious and timeless sense of exploration of one another's bodies, touching, kissing, caressing and playing with each other in ways that awaken all the senses. Introduce massage into your relationship, because then you can develop your tactile sensitivity with each other, responding to one another's needs with a skillful touch that can relax, invigorate, soothe away tension and pain, and enhance the sensuality of your physical relationship.

The arts of sensuality

The original *Kama Sutra* discusses the acts of embracing, kissing, and even biting and scratching in detail, regarding them all as sensual arts of love. It states that these things are generally done before sexual intercourse takes place, in other words as part of seduction and foreplay. However, it wisely

adds, *'Anything may take place at any time, for love does not care for time or order.'*

The precise way in which the text details different methods of embracing, kissing, scratching, and biting is in some respects rather superfluous, since most lovers hardly proceed with any of these acts as if by rote. However, these act descriptions do make it clear that there is an art to these practises, that it is highly varied, and that much is conveyed between lovers by body language and different modes of sensual touching.

Embracing

Included in embracing are hugs, cuddles and full body embraces that you share with your partner on meeting, in moments of intimacy and passion, and during foreplay. How you embrace each other may depend on your own attitudes towards sensuality and touching. An embrace may be nothing more than two bodies colliding or meeting briefly, or it can be the delight of two people uniting as if their bodies are melting together. The best way to dissolve into your embrace is to let go of your thoughts and your personal agenda and to bring your whole attention towards relaxing your body. We all carry some kind of body armour, or muscular tension, which acts as a means of protecting ourselves from inner and outer emotional stress, and this can make us stiff and unyielding, even in the arms of someone we love. By focusing your attention towards your senses and your body, and by breathing deeply, you can bring yourself more totally into the warm experience of the embrace.

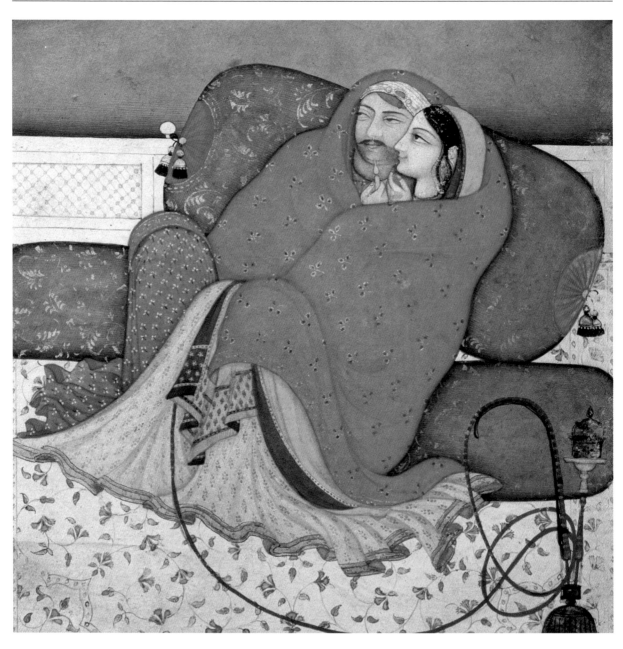

Encourage your partner to relax with you, because when two people hold each other closely and breathe together there can be a harmonious exchange of energy which feels as if you are merging together. This creates the opportunity for both of you to become more receptive to one another, and more in touch with your feelings.

The *Kama Sutra* describes, among others, four particular kinds of embrace which lovers can enjoy. They are as follows.

Jataveshtitaka, The Twining of a Creeper

This embrace focuses on the woman's actions as she entwines herself around her lover "as a creeper twines around a tree." She gently pulls his head down towards hers with the obvious desire to kiss him, and to initiate a tender and sensual exchange between them. The woman's desire will inevitably be expressed by an audible sound, probably caused by her deep inhalation of breath or her sighing. While this description pictures the woman in a clinging posture, she is obviously taking the lead in seducing her man.

Vriskshadhirudhaka, Climbing a Tree

Again, the woman takes control of the action, drawing her lover closer to her by placing her foot against his foot and wrapping her other leg against

This 18th-century Hindu painting shows two lovers in an intimate embrace as they recline on a couch in their love nest.

The terms for various embraces in the Kama Sutra *are imaginatively descriptive. The 'twining of a creeper' illustrated above involves the woman entwining herself cosily around her man.*

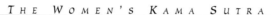

When lovers embrace, with limbs interlocked, and rub their bodies together in close contact, it is known as the 'mixture of sesame seed with rice'.

the back of one of his thighs. She also puts one arm around his back and the other on his shoulder while she makes "singing and cooing" sounds. Although the woman looks ready to climb up her lover's body, she is actually pulling his body closer to her breasts and genitals, and is giving him clear signals that she is willing for their embrace to become more intimate. A modern woman is likely to be more direct in her intentions, using well-chosen words to clearly indicate her desire, rather than billing and cooing in the manner suggested by the *Kama Sutra*. However, passion can indeed express itself most eloquently in sound, sighs, and audible breaths, and it is a language well understood by lovers.

Tila-tandulaka,
The Mixture of Sesame Seed with Rice

This embrace and the next describe the deepening passion of lovers who are ready to engage in sexual intercourse. Lying on a bed, the two lovers' limbs are so closely entwined it is as if all parts of their bodies are being rubbed together. The *Kama Sutra* describes this embrace as "the mixture of sesame seed with rice," an image of seed and grain being ground together in the typical mortar and pestle fashion of Hindu cuisine. Hugging and cuddling like this will help to release tensions in both the bodies and minds of the lovers. Such an embrace can become very playful, with lovers rolling around together on the bed, peppering their hugs and kisses with playful bites. The rubbing together of intimate body parts, such as the breasts, thighs, and pubic area will arouse erotic feelings and awaken the senses, so that the lovers are ready for any ensuing act of sexual intercourse.

Kshiraniraka, The Milk and Water Embrace

If you pour water into milk the two liquids combine; their separateness dissolves so that they are no longer two different substances but form part of each other. The "milk and water" embrace is the essential Tantric embrace of lovers whereby a man and woman melt together on an energetic level, so that for a period of time it is as if they are one body and mind. This is an embrace born out of deep intimacy and trust where both partners, holding each other and breathing together, have let go of their own egos and connect as one being.

It can be a deeply intimate moment when two people kiss as a gesture of affection, love and sexual attraction.

An embrace such as this brings a transcendental quality to lovemaking, though it can be done with or without coital penetration with the woman sitting on the man's lap or the couple lying in a supine or side-by-side position. Holding one another in stillness and silence in this way will engender a meditative quality in any ensuing lovemaking.

The art of kissing

Kissing can be simply a symbol of affection and greeting or it can be a deeply erotic experience, as pleasurable and intimate as making love. In ancient Hindu and Tantric texts, the kiss was considered to be a very significant act between lovers as the mingling of the body juices through saliva

was believed to harmonize the polar energies of the man and woman. So intimate was the sexual kiss considered to be that until very recently in India it was forbidden to show kissing in films and a husband and wife would never kiss publicly. In the West, kissing is a far more public affair, shown explicitly in films and on television, and acted out by passionate lovers in streets and parks without inhibition.

A lover's kiss remains a very intimate activity, for it does involve the exchange of body fluids and inevitably excites strong sexual feelings. Yet kissing is not purely a physical activity, for the manner in which kissing takes place transmits the deeper emotional feelings of the two people concerned. Kissing is certainly one of the major arts of love, and a good lover is one who has learnt to kiss with both subtlety and force, tenderness and passion. The lips and tongue become instruments of seduction and love, willing to worship not just the mouth but the whole body of the beloved.

A tell-tale kiss

A woman can probably gain a good insight into the potential lovemaking skills of a new partner by the manner in which he kisses her. A man who approaches her mouth too directly, with tense lips

> **"Kissing is of four kinds: moderate, contracted, pressed and soft, according to the different parts of the body which are being kissed. Different types of kisses are appropriate for different parts of the body."**

and a tongue which intrudes too quickly, is unlikely to be a sensitive lover given to the pleasures of foreplay. He may very well treat her *yoni* in a similar way, penetrating too fast and without care for her arousal. If his methods of kissing are limited and repetitive, it is likely that his thrusting movements during intercourse will also lack flexibility and imagination.

The momentum to a truly sensual kiss should build up slowly in the same way that good lovemaking does. The *Kama Sutra* talks about kissing the forehead, the eyes, the cheeks, and the throat. Being kissed like this, where each part of the face is caressed by the lips, builds passion steadily and allows time for both people to become emotionally receptive to each other. Those kisses, planted tenderly on the face, convey a sense of deep affection as well as sexual attraction. When their mouths finally meet the lovers are more in harmony, so that lips and tongue eagerly seek each other, interacting spontaneously between being active and passive, gentle and passionate without clashing or awkwardness.

Rodin's sculpture The Kiss *depicts the passion of lovers involved in a deeply intimate kiss.*

Taste and smell

Kissing is a good way to immediately gauge the physical compatibility between yourself and the man you are attracted to. While his appearance and manner may be pleasing to you, the close encounter of a full kiss will quickly reveal if the chemistry is right between you. Taste and smell are two of the most important senses engaged in sexual compatibility and both are immediately activated by kissing. While visual attraction can be influenced by mental images of what constitutes the "right" look, taste and smell provoke an authentic bodily response. For most animals these senses drive the sexual attraction factor, but as human beings we are less aware of such instinctive forces until a full mouth-to-mouth kiss brings us directly in contact with them. Even if the man concerned is perfect in looks and actions, take heed of the immediate signals your body will give you on receiving that first kiss.

Good oral hygiene is, of course, essential to the art of kissing. No matter how sexy someone is, it is simply impossible to enjoy a kiss that carries the stale flavour of someone's last meal or reeks of cigarette smoke. Keep your mouth clean and fresh by brushing your teeth after each meal and using dental floss regularly. Bad breath may also be caused by chronic gum disease or digestive problems, so if you think your breath smells unpleasant it is advisable to seek dental or medical advice.

Supple lips

Exercise your face muscles daily to keep your mouth flexible and relaxed so that your lips remain supple and ready to kiss and be kissed. The face, and in particular the area of the mouth and jaw, can store a lot of tension. Our faces presents our images to the world, and in a struggle to control emotions which would otherwise reveal themselves clearly we unconsciously tighten the facial muscles. Each morning, make funny faces in the mirror, screw up your eyes, purse your lips, widen your mouth, and move your jaw from side to side to help release the tension. In addition, these simple exercises can help to keep the face well contoured.

Creative kissing

Mouths, lips and tongues can play endlessly and creatively with each other, so that the kissing portrays a variety of feelings and sexual impulses. One or both lips can be embraced within a kiss. The tongue can travel softly over the outline of the lips, or gently enter the soft interior of the mouth. When kissing becomes more intense and passionate, the lovers' tongues may penetrate deeply into one another's mouths, taking it in turns to explore and caress.

The activity of kissing belongs equally to the man and woman. The *Kama Sutra* states: "Whatever things may be done by one of the lovers to the other, the same should be returned by the other. If the woman kisses him, he should kiss her in return." It describes various methods of kissing. First it talks about the way in which a man should kiss a young or inexperienced woman. However, in the initial stages of a relationship, even an experienced woman may feel tentative and bashful and may appreciate a respectful and gentle approach. For these tender occasions when two people are just beginning to know each other, the *Kama Sutra* suggests the following modes of kissing:

The 'touching kiss' is enacted when the woman shyly brushes the man's lips with her tongue.

The Nominal Kiss

This is the very first kiss, where affection is being demonstrated but the action is not intended to arouse sexual feelings. The woman accepts a kiss on the mouth, but does not actively return it.

The Throbbing Kiss

Once familiarity has been established the woman may wish to respond a little to the kiss, but without initiating too much passion. As the man kisses her mouth, she moves only her lower lip.

The Touching Kiss

The woman cautiously intimates that she is willing to let the relationship become more intimate. Here she closes her eyes in response to being kissed and strokes the man's lips with her tongue, while taking his hands into her own.

The *Kama Sutra* then goes on to describe other types of kisses, presumably for those who have begun to establish a sexual relationship.

The Straight Kiss

The mouths of the lovers meet in full contact with each other, without any hesitation or embarrassment.

The Bent Kiss

With heads held at an angle, the lovers' lips meet comfortably without the awkward collision of noses. In this position, full and passionate kissing can easily ensue.

The Turned Kiss

With this kiss, the taller partner lifts the other's face towards their own by tilting the chin upwards with their hand. It is a tender gesture that will generate a sweet exchange of kisses.

Lifting the woman's chin gently upwards, the man performs 'the turned kiss'.

Pressed Kisses

More force and passion are used in these kisses. The "pressed kiss" occurs when one lover catches the lower lip of the other between their own lips and presses it firmly. The "greatly pressed kiss" is even more erotic, for the lover first takes the lower lip of the other between the fingers, then caresses it with the tongue, then catches it between the lips and presses it with force.

The 'kiss of the upper lip'. This kiss occurs when one lover kisses the upper lip while the other kisses the lower lip.

The Clasping Kiss

This is a passionate kiss, such as one that might occur during the height of sexual arousal. One lover takes the lips of the other fully between their own, and penetrates the tongue into the mouth, stroking it against the other's tongue, teeth and palate.

Fighting of the Tongue

This is the equivalent to the modern-day "French kiss". The tongues of both lovers seek each other out, rolling sensually against each other, sometimes gently and sometimes with force. If this is happening during coitus, it is exciting to let the movements synchronize with the thrusting and pelvic motions.

A Kiss That Kindles Love

Every woman who loves a man will know this kiss. She gazes on her lover's face as he sleeps beside her, then kisses it gently. She hopes he will awaken from his slumber and respond to her desire for him.

A Kiss That Turns Away

This is the kiss employed by a woman to distract her lover away from other tasks. She might use it to soften his hardened heart during a quarrel. The kiss is an invitation to him to forget everything else that is happening and to give her some loving attention.

Kiss That Awakens

Here the woman awaits late at night for her lover to return. She feigns indifference by going to bed, but she is only pretending to sleep. When her man arrives, she secretly waits for him to kiss her in an attempt to 'awaken' her. In this way, she gains a clear idea of his intention and desire for her.

The tender kiss of a woman as her partner sleeps is known as the kiss that kindles love.

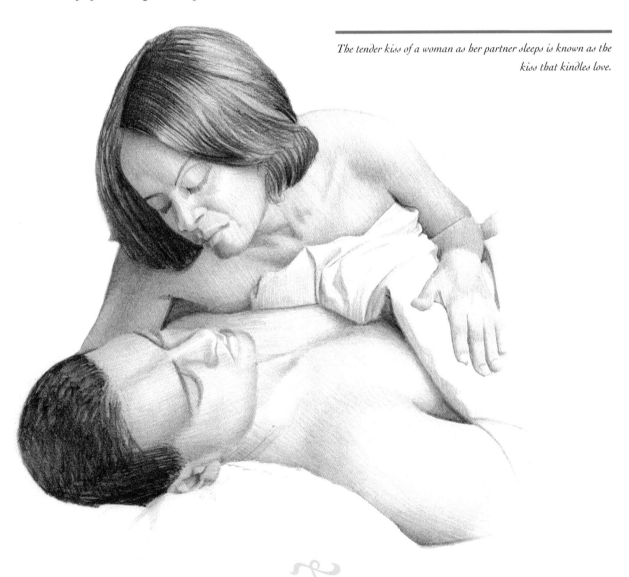

The marks of love

In spite of this statement, the _Kama Sutra_ does admit that only some women like scratching and biting during sex, and those are usually only women of a passionate nature. Such sexual practises, says the book, are likely to occur mostly on certain occasions, such as on the first amorous encounter, when a lover is going away or just returning from a journey, when lovers reconcile after a fight, or when the woman is intoxicated.

Scratching and biting, therefore, is part of 'hot' sex, when one or both lovers become uninhibited during an erotic escapade, and in an almost animalistic way start to mark their claim on their sexual partner. Generally, scratching and biting during sex is more likely to be done by a woman to a man, rather than vice versa. Perhaps it is one way a female can physically demonstrate her power with the man when lust runs wild. She might scratch his back with her nails, or sink her teeth into his skin. However passionately she feels, she needs to take care not to break the skin and cause bleeding. Some men will love this wild display of passion from their partners, while others may feel slightly intimidated by it.

> **When a woman sees the marks of nails on the private parts of her body, even if they are old and almost worn out, then her love becomes fresh and new.**

Love bites

Love bites, where the skin is actually sucked rather than bitten, can prove unsightly and embarrassing once the heat of passion wears off, the purplish-blue marks remaining visible for some time. It is unlikely that a modern woman would want to flaunt these marks, particularly in her workplace, so it is better to avoid such marks on an area of the body which is exposed publicly, such as the neck.

Yet a small love bite, or love scratch, hidden on a private part of the body, will act as an aphrodisiac to the mind when the lovers are parted. There is something most exciting about presenting a respectable almost asexual face to the world, such as at a business meeting, while knowing that on your breast or thigh there remains a symbol of a night of passion. However, as the _Kama Sutra_ wisely warns, if either a man or woman is engaged in an adulterous affair it is better to leave no trace of love marks, except in the most hidden places.

Variety is spice

The detailed description that the _Kama Sutra_ gives to the varying types of bites and scratches that lovers can inflict on each other demonstrates that such acts were once considered skillful arts of love. It would seem they were a more popular practise in

---

When a lover passionately bites the other on the shoulder, and leaves teeth marks, it is termed by the Kama Sutra _as 'the biting of the boar'._

the ancient East than in the modern West. These practices do, however, introduce variety to lovemaking and, as the *Kama Sutra* says, "If variety is sought in all the arts and amusements, how much more should it be sought after in the art of love."

Sounding with the Nails

The nails are drawn all over the skin of the body, including the most intimate areas such as breasts and thighs. The pressure is soft enough to leave no mark, but the movement of the nails makes a sound, and the nerve endings of the skin are tantalized so that the body hair becomes erect.

Half Moon

By pushing the nails into the skin, a crescent-shaped mark like a half moon is created. Such symbols can be made on the neck and breasts or the man's chest.

A Line

Perhaps the most common of love scratches, these are the straight nail marks left on a man's back by the woman's nails.

The Hidden Bite

This is the love bite, often favoured by young lovers, on the neck, bosom and chest. It causes an excessive redness in the skin, which is either sucked or bitten.

Biting of the Boar

This, says the *Kama Sutra*, is the mark of people of great passion. It is usually placed on the shoulder or breast, and is caused by broad rows of teeth-marks close to each other.

Coral and Jewel

This bite is formed by pressure from the lips and teeth and is usually placed on the cheek, but could also be appropriate for the buttocks. The lips are perceived as coral and the teeth as jewels.

Perhaps the most common love scratches, known as 'a line', are the straight nail marks left on a man's back by a woman's nails.

Sensual foreplay

In the ancient Eastern texts on sexuality, men were taught to know and enjoy the skills of sensual foreplay to enhance not only the woman's pleasure but also their own. Yet this understanding of the joys of sensuality appears to have been somewhat lost over the following centuries, possibly because certain cultures and religions became oppressive towards sexuality and, in particular, towards the exuberant orgasmic nature of women. Until more recent times, and in some cases even to this day, some men seem to have little understanding of the role

> " The whole subject of embracing is of such nature that men who ask questions about it, or who hear about it, or who talk about it, acquire thereby a desire for enjoyment. "

of sensuality in lovemaking. Nor do they seem to know how important it is to a woman's arousal response, and to her sexual and emotional satisfaction. Indeed, some men appear to have no idea how sensual touching in foreplay can improve their own sexual pleasure.

A man who knows how to touch and caress a woman in a sensual manner can easily win her heart.

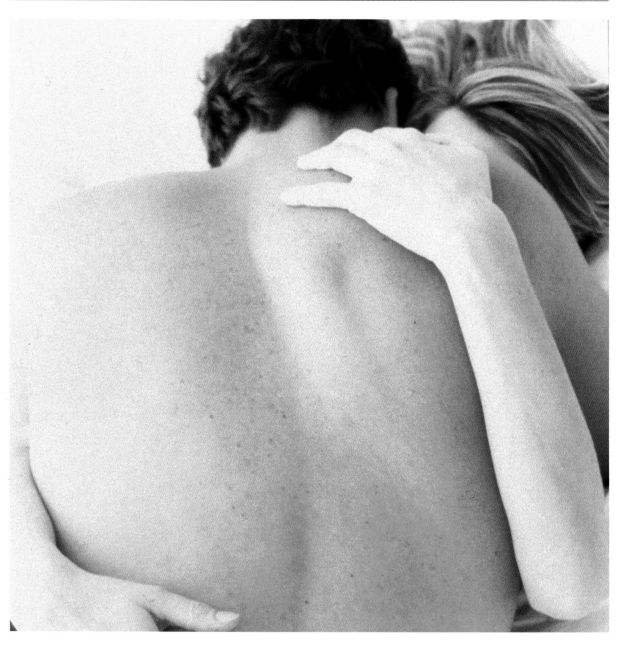

Of course, there have always been men who are naturally sensual and instinctively good lovers, and who delight in all manner of tender and passionate methods of foreplay. Recent research shows that for the majority of modern men, their greatest pleasure in lovemaking is to see that the woman reaches her own peak of sexual happiness. Men have become more enlightened about women's sexuality over the last decades because of the frank discussions in all forms of the media regarding women's sexual needs and orgasmic potential. Women also have become more informed and able to ask for what they need to attain sexual satisfaction.

Understanding sensuality

The importance of sensuous foreplay and whole body touching, and the role of the clitoris in a woman's orgasmic arousal, are all commonly available knowledge for any man who wants to be a caring lover. Knowing about sensuality and being sensual, however, are two entirely different things. Some men still get it badly wrong. Rather than relaxing into sensuality for its own sake and for the mutual enjoyment of both lovers, some men "do" things to their female partners in order to get the "right" response. They focus their attention on the breasts or clitoris, aware that these are both highly erogenous areas in women. But most women find it

Lovemaking is enhanced by the intimate foreplay that proceeds it and the pleasure that lovers take in simply touching and enjoying one another's bodies.

irritating and unsatisfying if these intimate parts of the body are rubbed, tweaked and sucked in an obvious effort to gain a result. What turns a woman on is whole body sensuality, and seeing her man lose himself in the pleasure of adorning her body with loving caresses, licks, and kisses. In sensual foreplay there is no schedule and no time limit; it is playful, luxurious, erotic and, most essentially, mutually satisfying.

A sensual man who can enjoy endless foreplay, who loves to give and receive pleasure in this way, and who is not in a terrific hurry to penetrate his partner, is one who probably feels good about his own body and has a deep appreciation of women generally. He does not differentiate between her pleasure and his, for he knows that sexual happiness is a voyage of discovery undertaken by two people.

Enlighten him

If your man is shy or inexperienced in the arts of love, you can enlighten him on the skills of foreplay in a loving, playful, and patient manner. Make love to him in the way that you would like him to make love to you. Ask him to let you take the lead, and refrain from rushing into intercourse. He should become the passive partner while you cover his body with your kisses, caress his skin with your tongue, and brush your hair and breasts against him provocatively. Draw his focus away from his genital area, which is his most highly charged erogenous zone, so that he begins to enjoy the subtle sensations of pleasure he can experience all over his body.

No part of his body is unworthy of your attention. Nibble his ears and kiss his neck. Move your lips slowly and tantalizingly down his body. Suck and kiss his nipples and let your tongue explore and discover his special erogenous areas. Cup your hands under his buttocks and kiss and lick his belly and thighs.

Stroke down his legs and kiss, lick, or suck his toes. Ask him to turn over and then caress the back of his body. The buttocks are an erogenous zone, especially for men, and he will find pleasure in you stroking and squeezing them. All the time you are building up his arousal, yet at the same time you are relaxing him emotionally. You are drawing him into the whole sensuality of touch and foreplay. Do not overstimulate your partner so that he ejaculates too quickly; the whole point of this sensual adventure is to encourage him to relax into foreplay, and to experience it as an extra dimension to the joy of lovemaking.

What your partner should understand is that foreplay is not just about sexual arousal but it also a way for lovers to relax deeply with one another's bodies, to enhance their senses and erotic responses, and to become more open and emotionally trusting with each other. The *Kama Sutra* encourages this kind of whole body foreplay, advising lovers to embrace the thighs, the breasts, and the pubic area and to let their kisses adorn the forehead, eyes, cheeks, throat, bosom, arms, belly, thighs, and genital areas.

Female arousal

In the beginning of coitus, the passion of a woman is middling, and she cannot bear the vigorous thrusts of her lover; but by degrees her passion increases until she ceases to think about her body.

Most women need loving foreplay to become sufficiently sexually aroused to reach their orgasmic potential. While no two women's sexual responses are identical, it is generally true that a woman needs more time than a man to be ready for penetrative sex. Also, the woman's whole body is more naturally erogenous than a man's. She can be erotically thrilled by the tenderest kiss to her face, his lips against her nipples, his caresses against her legs and arms, his tongue lovingly exploring her clitoris. When a man is attentive to a woman in this way, embracing and kissing her all over with no haste or goal in mind but relishing every inch of her body, her trust in his regard for her grows and her full sexuality unfolds like a bud under the warmth of the sun. As her arousal intensifies, her vaginal juices begin to flow and she becomes ready emotionally and physically to receive her lover inside herself. A woman whose whole body is erotically awakened through sensual foreplay can be truly orgasmic.

Sensuality throughout lovemaking

All the arts of love described above, which are perfect for attaining harmony and arousal before lovemaking, should be continued during sexual intercourse. The word "foreplay" can be misleading because it suggests that the tactile activities which aid arousal should come before coitus, while in fact they are part of the whole act of lovemaking. Kissing, caressing, and embracing will ensure that intimacy and tenderness continue throughout love-making, so that the couple will stay emotionally and physically attuned. Eye contact and the exchange of loving words will also enhance their pleasure.

In those fragile moments after intercourse and orgasm, lovers should take care not to lose their close connection with each other. At this point the post-coital response of the man and woman can be very different, and if the couple are not sensitive to one another's needs the compatibility of their love-making can be shattered. After ejaculating, a man may feel temporarily depleted of energy. This is the refractory phase of a man's orgasmic cycle, and a woman should respect her partner's need to rest. By contrast, woman may feel full of energy after making love. She may even want to continue to have sex, or at least to receive her partner's attention. However, a wise woman will refrain from being too demanding at this time, encouraging her partner instead to relax in the warm embrace of her arms.

In this situation, the man should never cut himself off emotionally from his partner. Men who do this may be afraid of the intense intimacy of the situation, or their own sense of powerlessness and vulnerability. No woman appreciates a lover who immediately rolls over and falls asleep after his orgasm, and indeed the woman may feel deeply rejected.

Lying closely entwined is restful for both partners after their sexual activity. It allows time for their energies to be replenished, while maintaining a nurturing sense of harmony and intimacy between them.

The *Kama Sutra* describes eloquently the affection that lovers can share in the afterglow of love-making. It says that the man should anoint the woman's body with pure sandalwood ointment or some other sensual essence. He should embrace her, and bring her refreshments of food and drink. It urges the lovers to sit outside and contemplate the moon, and to talk intimately and agreeably with each other. In other words, the wise book urges men and women to put as much tenderness and affection into the period after making love as they did before and during it.

The art of massage

Some say that even shampooing is a kind of embrace, because there is a touching of bodies in it. But Vatsyayana thinks that shampooing is performed at a different time, and for a different purpose; and as it is also of a different character, it cannot be said to be included in the embrace.

"Shampooing" is the ancient term for massage and the *Kama Sutra* suggests that as a form to tactile contact it has a different purpose and character to the sexual embrace. Massage, of course, does play a vital role in enhancing the affection and sensuality of a relationship and it can become an erotic experience, its rhythmic strokes relaxing the mind while sensitizing the skin and bringing alive the body's responses. However, massage serves many purposes, not only the sexual relationship. Loving, attentive hands on the body can heal and soothe the spirit, reduce stress, alleviate pain, boost the cardiovascular system and calm the nerves; they can restore self-esteem, well-being and equilibrium while promoting a wholesome sense of body image. Massage can be as sensual, as intimate and as fulfilling as making love. As such, the exchanges of massage within a relationship provide a deeply satisfying alternative to lovemaking, especially at times when intercourse is not desired or advisable. Massage can also be part of lovemaking – a wonderful, loving way to prepare the body for the sensual delights to follow.

Becoming tactile

Touch, through the medium of massage, is a profound form of communication. It is a perfectly natural way for one person to reach out and respond to another, but society places many taboos on touching, especially when it occurs outside a recognized sexual relationship. This inhibition about touching, and the sexual connotations attached to it, means that many people lack confidence in their ability to touch another person. They are literally "out of touch." Physical contact which expresses concern, regard, warmth, and affection in an asexual way becomes hesitant or even ceases to exist in its own right.

Women are generally more likely to touch and pamper their bodies, and to spontaneously kiss, stroke, and embrace their intimate circle of family and friends, regardless of gender. This greater ease with physical contact means that most women enjoy touching and being touched for its own sensual sake. Men tend to be more inhibited and less tender than women in their manner of touching, but this lack of tactile subtlety is usually more to do with conditioning that aptitude. In Western cultures, men are not encouraged to demonstrate physical affection towards each other – hence all the brisk backslapping on greeting even close friends and relatives of the same gender. Touching someone of the opposite sex is also fraught with tension because of the obvious association with sexuality. Enjoying massage as a regular feature in a relationship is certainly one of the best methods for both men and women to gain confidence and ease in their manner of touching.

Exchanging massages

To give a massage to your lover is as rewarding and creative an experience as receiving one, especially once you have become confident with the techniques and strokes. Knowledge of massage, then, is definitely one of the arts of love and should be added to your repertoire of relationship skills. Do introduce it as an additional resource of pleasure, relaxation, sensuality, and when appropriate, as a luxurious form of foreplay.

There are many books available from which you can learn the techniques of massage. Set up some regular massage practise times with a friend, or your partner, and experiment with the strokes. Join a massage class where you can learn, in a support-

Massage can both relax and revive the body and mind. Used within a relationship, it introduces a new dimension of emotional and physical closeness.

ive environment, how to construct a flowing, full body massage. Persuade your man to come with you and learn together how to use your hands to relax the body with soft, rhythmic motions, and how to deftly squeeze and knead muscles to relieve tension. Once you have mastered the basic techniques, and are confident in the capabilities of your hands, you can then let your intuition and spontaneity guide your strokes.

Overcoming reluctance

What should you do if your man loves to receive massage from you but is less than enthusiastic or adept at returning the favour? First, be patient and find out the reasons behind his reluctance, or why the quality of his touch feels unsatisfactory. Do not criticize him too hastily, but rather give constructive feedback. Your partner's touch may be hesitant because he is concerned that his pressure is too strong for you. Perhaps his touch is a little bit rough and speedy. Do not take this lack of tactile sensitivity to be a reflection of his regard for you, but ask him to experiment with varying degrees of pressure and speed as he massages you, then praise him when the weight, depth, and pace of the strokes feel good. If you encourage your partner he will grow increasingly confident in his ability to touch sensually.

A fun way to banish the stresses of the day and to relax together in the evening is to give each other a shoulder massage.

Massage your lover frequently so that you demonstrate through your strokes just how you liked to be touched. Treat him to some professional holistic massage sessions where therapeutic techniques are combined with a healing, relaxing touch. The more relaxed he becomes with this sensitive level of tactile contact, the more he will appreciate the wonderful sense of whole-body integration that ensues from it. He will learn that firm hands can also be gentle; that a deep stroke can be a relaxing one; and that tactile sensuality has a wondrous life of its own other than being solely an adjunct to sex. His increased understanding of the depth and range of tactile communication will enrich your relationship.

Once you both feel confident about giving and receiving message, let it become a precious means through which you demonstrate your caring and love for each other. If one of you is suffering from stress, the other can soothe away the tensions with a deeply relaxing full body message. It is better that one of you takes the active role while the other simply receives the message; an exchange can be arranged for another time. Short massages are also an attractive option. For example, when one of you returns home from work with a headache, the other can alleviate the stress with a 20-minute shoulder, neck and head message. You can even exchange a pampering foot massage at the end of a wearying day, or before going to sleep.

The cycle of giving and receiving

Massage allows you to become intimate and familiar with every inch of your lover's body. When receiving a massage, open yourself up wholly to your partner's touch. If you are giving the massage, pour yourself totally into your hands. Allow this mutual exchange of giving and receiving to become an unbroken cycle of energy flowing between you. Once the massage is functioning intuitively from your heart, rather than from your mind, you may feel as if you are merging energetically with one another. This feeling of oneness offers you a glimpse into that same sense of union which arises during meditative lovemaking.

Erotic massage

An erotic massage can be a wonderful prelude to sexual intercourse when that is its mutually desired intention. Your strokes can release your partner's mind and body from tension while stimulating the

> **She occupies herself with shampooing his body and pressing his head. When shampooing him, she works with one hand only, and with the other she touches and embraces parts of his body. She remains with both hands placed on his body motionless, as if she had been surprised by something or was overcome by fatigue.**
>
> **She sometimes bends her face down upon his thighs, and when asked to shampoo them does not manifest any unwillingness to do so. She places one of her hands quite motionless on his body, and even though the man should press it between two members of his body, she does not remove it for a long time.**

senses and erotic responses. First, prepare a welcoming and womb-like atmosphere in the room where you are to give the massage. The room should be warm, well-ventilated and draught-free. Keep a small stock of clean fresh towels and sheets close by to cover your lover should he start to get cold. If you intend to give a full body massage, set the mattress, cushions or blankets on floor level to provide a supportive base. Your bed may look inviting as a location for massage, but the softness of the mattress will not necessarily provide sufficient support for either of you during the movement of massage. Scatter cushions and pillows around your massage space to kneel on, or to place beneath parts of your partner's body for comfort.

Prepare the room lovingly before giving a massage. A warm environment, infused with aroma and softly lit, will ensure a sensual and relaxing experience for both of you.

Use low, warm lighting in the room to create a romantic ambience. Longlasting candles will provide a soft purity of light and cast flattering shadows on the skin – but keep them a safe distance away from your massage area. Select beforehand some of your favourite music to play during the massage. The music should be evocative and relaxing, but the rhythm must not be intrusive.

Fragrant oils for massage

Prepare a blend of message oil using aromatic essences to enhance the erotic and romantic mood of your sensual massage. The essential oils may be selected for the purpose of being uplifting, relaxing, balancing, warming, mentally inspiring, spiritually elevating, and erotically enhancing. (See pages 24–26 for information on the properties of specific essential oils.) Choose essences whose aromas are pleasing to your partner. Mix this fragrant blend with a basic oil such as grapeseed, sunflower, sweet almond, jobojobo or avocado and pour into a porcelain or glass bowl or bottle. Use around 1 fl oz (25ml) of carrier oil for a whole body massage, and to this add about 12 drops of essential oils. Mix no more than three different essences for any one recipe, ensuring that their fragrances and qualities are complementary and are certain to heighten the pleasure of a sensual massage.

Aromatic essential oils distilled from plants and herbs will enhance the romantic mood of the massage when added, according to instruction, to the basic carrier oil.

If you prefer not to mix the essential oils with the basic oil, pour some drops instead into an aromatherapy burner so that their heady and potent scent disperses into the room.

Before the massage, invite your lover into a candlelit bathroom to bathe or shower with you. Soap his body, using your hands to knead away tension from his shoulders and neck. After the bath, dry his body with a warm, soft towel and lead him into the massage area which has been lovingly prepared by you. Ask him to lie, face down, on the mattress and then kneel beside him.

Flowing strokes

A flowing stroke is done by sliding the flat of both hands together in a steady motion up or down over an area of the body before fanning your hands outwards to the sides of the body and gliding them back to the start of the stroke. This soothing motion can be repeated several times and is relaxing and warming to the tissues.

Kneading strokes

Kneading strokes wring the muscles and follow an action similar to that of a baker kneading dough. They are invigorating motions which release tension and loosen tight areas of muscle. Scoop, wring and roll the flesh in one hand before passing it over to the other hand. In an unbroken rhythm, pass the flesh back and forth between both hands, working thoroughly over a muscular area such as the buttocks, thighs or shoulders.

How to begin

Place a little oil in the palms of your hands and begin to spread it over the whole surface of his back and legs, sweeping your hands over his body in a flowing manner. Let your hands be as fluid and supple as a sculptor's, accentuating the contours of his body as they glide over them. Begin your massage on his back, alternating rhythmically between soft, sliding strokes which warm and enliven his skin and deeper, more kneading motions in areas of tension such as his shoulders and buttocks. Your man will especially enjoy the stronger action on his buttocks.

Left: warm the oil or lotion between your palms before spreading it evenly over the skin with flowing and steady strokes. Focus your attention into your hands.

Skin sensations

Straddle his hips, hugging the sides of his body between your thighs. As your hands sweep up the length of his back, lower your body so that your breasts and belly brush his skin. If you have long hair, let it trail on to his back. Create different skin sensations for him, drawing your nails or feather-touching your fingertips down his spine and blowing your warm breath lightly on his body.

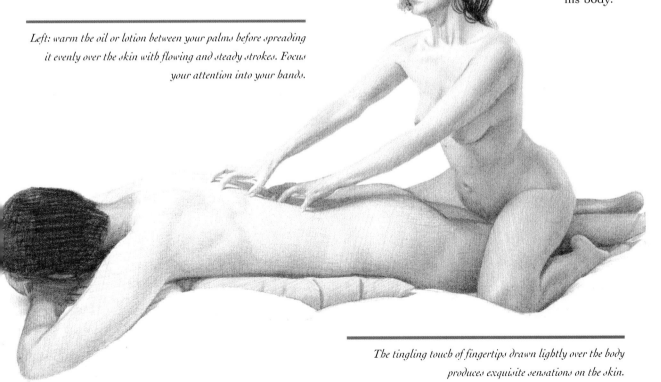

The tingling touch of fingertips drawn lightly over the body produces exquisite sensations on the skin.

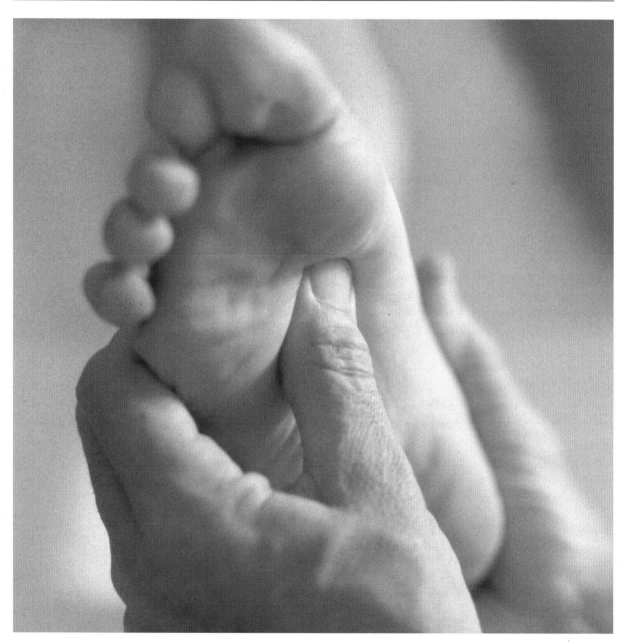

Legs and feet

In this way, continue your massage down the back of his legs, adding oil to your hands whenever the skin needs extra lubrication. Slide your hand frequently between his thighs, without stopping for too long on his intimate area. Move to his feet, lifting them one at a time to rest on your knees. Press firmly all over the soles of his feet with your thumbs and pull gently on his toes. Then run your little finger into the soft folds of skin between each toe – this can feel very sexy.

When you have massaged the back of your man's body, ask him to turn over. Start at his feet and work your sensual strokes up the front of his legs, focusing special attention on his thighs and letting your strokes caress his loins and *lingam*.

The front of his body

Kneel at the side of his body and, using the flat of your hands, make sweeping circular movement over the softness of his belly. Straddle his body again, and massage his chest, your strokes embracing its full circumference. Again you can lower your body close to his so that he feels just the barest touch of your nipples on his skin. Do not forget to massage his arms and hands as this is an often neglected area and he will appreciate having the tension massaged away. When his hands are relaxed, put his fingertips one by one into your mouth and suck then gently.

Head and neck

Now position yourself behind your partner's head and take it gently on your lap. Knead the back of his shoulders and neck with your fingertips and create a gentle friction all over his scalp with tiny shampooing finger motions. Pour your love into your hands as you massage his face, letting your strokes be sensitive but also firm and steady. Follow the structure of his facial features, moving down from the forehead to the jaw. Gently run a fingertip over his lips and softly over his closed eyes. Complete the massage by stroking your fingers tenderly through his hair.

When the massage is complete, snuggle down beside your lover and allow the feelings that are there between you to take over.

A foot massage can relieve tension from the whole body, leaving your partner feeling refreshed and revitalised. Combine with strokes over the legs for a real treat.

CHAPTER FIVE

The Kama Sutra Arts of Love

" By union with men,
the lust, desire, or passion
of women is satisfied,
and the pleasure derived
from the consciousness of it is
called their satisfaction. **"**

*E*very woman knows in her heart that it is the quality of feeling and the rapport between lovers rather than any technique that makes sexual intercourse so satisfying. No performance, no matter how finely tuned, can compensate for the fire of desire and the tenderness of touch which flows when two bodies unite in spontaneous passion and love. Then the spirit dances freely within the body, liberating the lovers to move easily and gracefully from one position to another, to explore and experiment, and to naturally and without inhibition abandon sexual conventions and boundaries. In such an atmosphere, every breath taken together, every sweet caress, is savoured for its own exquisite pleasure in that moment rather than as a means of reaching some other goal in the next.

*L*ove positions

Women can quickly sense when lovemaking techniques, no matter how polished their execution, are of a mechanical nature. A gymnastic performance in bed and a cleverly orchestrated orgasm cannot substitute for the feeling of being cared for and loved. Such sexual activity has a hollow ring to it, as if the body has been taken but the soul and the emotions have been left behind. Yet knowledge of a variety of lovemaking techniques keeps a sexual relationship vibrant and prevents it slipping into monotonous routines. It is like taking a well-loved song and adding new harmonies and notes to it to keep the music constantly alive and creative.

This chapter looks at frank descriptions of sexual choices, but from a more feminine perspective than the original *Kama Sutra*. Women, who for centuries were conditioned to believe that their only sexual role was to please a man in bed rather than seek their own fulfillment, should benefit from understanding how certain sexual positions work for both male and female satisfaction. Also, they need to know that they have choices which liberate them from the traditional male-dominated positions so that they too can be equal in orchestrating an active sexual life. A woman with knowledge about her own body and sexual needs can tactfully educate her man into becoming a more sensitive lover. In doing so, she can then reclaim her femininity, allowing her soft and passive nature to coexist harmoniously with her own powerful sexual drive.

Yet every contemporary woman who wants a longlasting and successful sexual relationship should also be aware of a man's sexual needs and vulnerabilities. In the same way she wants her desires fulfilled, so she should be sensitive to what makes her man happy. A joyful sex life, freed from the gender battlefield, will enrich a relationship. It is a mutual escape from the strains of modern life, functioning not only as an activity which safely releases stress but also as an ongoing source of physical, emotional, and spiritual nourishment. It is the meeting ground between man and woman, where their differences can be resolved, and their polarities harmonized. Good sex offers a constant source of renewal for a relationship – so here are a variety of the lovemaking techniques suggested in the *Kama Sutra*.

Intimate positions for lovemaking

Penetration in lovemaking should not occur until you are fully aroused, and feel ready, emotionally and physically, for your partner to enter you. At this stage, your vulva will plump up and your vagina will secrete its love juices. Emotionally, you will long for him to be inside you. Continue to caress and kiss each other, or indulge in some oral stimulation until the time is ripe for you. Beware of a man who is in too much of a hurry; encourage him to become more sensual, enjoying foreplay for its own sake and as an expression of his love for you, rather than as a means to speed up penetrative sex. A man who is insensitive in this way is one who does not understand the hearts of women and he is bound to make you unhappy sooner or later. When intercourse begins, he should enter you slowly. The Widely Opened Position described in chapter two is a suitable posture to adopt for easy penetration.

At the start of intercourse, take time to tune in to each other physically and emotionally so that you can both savour those first moments of intimate union before engaging in more vigorous activity. Throughout the duration of lovemaking, it is essential to remain connected to each other if it is to be a truly satisfying experience. The following intimate positions for coitus are perfect for allowing time and space for the exchanges of tenderness, and for harmonizing your energies so that you are making love as one rather than as two separate competitors in a single race. Do not be afraid to ask your lover to slow down for a while if you feel he is racing away from you amidst too much activity. The best way to regain connection is to return to an intimate lovemaking position, to have eye contact, to maintain whole body tactility and to take time to attune your breathing to each other.

The Clasping Position

A woman can feel very vulnerable as she receives her lover inside herself, and may need time to go through the transition stage from penetration to deep thrusting. There is no need to rush things. Lower your legs so the tip of the *lingam* can nestle snugly just inside your *yoni*, wrapped in the close fit of the lower vaginal muscles. This feeling is exciting, particularly as this area is packed with sensitive nerve endings. It will make your desire for deeper penetration all the more acute, allowing the upper canal of your vagina to naturally balloon out as a willing receptacle for your lover's member. Don't move your pelvis around too much at this time as too much stimulation now on the highly erogenous tip of the penis could cause your lover to ejaculate prematurely, leaving you both unsatisfied. The Clasping Position, described in the *Kama Sutra* as "when the legs of both the man and woman are stretched out straight over each other" is a perfect repose for this early stage of intercourse. It states that this position can be achieved by a couple lying in the supine or the side position, but the latter is better kept for a later stage of lovemaking when you and your lover want to rest between activity to assimilate the sensations of lovemaking and to deepen your intimacy before resuming movement.

The Pressing Position

This follows quite naturally from the Clasping Position. By closing your thighs against his legs, or against his penis, you tighten your vagina to hold the head of the penis snugly inside you, giving your partner time to moderate his ardour so that he does not rush, unheeding of you, towards his goalpost. Look into each other's eyes to remain emotionally connected, and continue to kiss and stroke each other – or close your eyes and focus your whole attention on the sensations within your vagina. Welcome him into yourself.

The Twining Position

When you are ready for further penetration, you should move from the Clasping into the Twining position by bending one leg across the back of his leg and nudging it up against his buttocks. Your lover will enjoy the pressure against his posterior and this movement will signal your willingness for him to enter you more deeply. You can also wrap your other leg around him, hugging him closer to you, and using your feet to caress his back.

Positions for passionate lovemaking

As your passion increases your uterus retracts, allowing space for deep thrusting from your partner. If, however, he penetrates you too hard and too fast, this can cause him to bang painfully against your cervix. Once you are ready for him, you will welcome the variety of his thrusts and enjoy engaging in positions which allow him to penetrate you fully. You will need to be fit and supple to remain comfortable in some of the deeply penetrative positions suggested in the *Kama Sutra*. Most of all, it helps to be flexible in your hip joints and thigh muscles. Yoga and stretch exercises will keep your body lithe and relaxed, while regular aerobic exercise will increase your stamina for lovemaking. Your man may particularly enjoy these positions for deep thrusting because they put him in control and make him feel potent and powerful. That gives you the opportunity to fall into the more passive side of your nature and it can be especially thrilling to willingly surrender your body to your lover; the fullness of his *lingam* thrusting within you can fill you with pleasure. In most of these positions, however, your own movements are restricted and you may tire of them easily. Also, the tipped position of your pelvis means that your clitoris, that tiny organ so vital to your sexual satisfaction, will receive little stimulation or contact with your partner's pubic bone. When you want to change from these positions to something more intimate, ask your lover to come close to you or to hold you tight.

Lovemaking positions such as the Rising and Yawning positions, appropriate for "high union," or for a woman with a narrow *yoni* making love to a well-endowed man, are obviously also suitable for deep penetration since they cause the woman's vagina to be widened and lengthened.

Hindu art is explicit in its depiction of sexual positions, many of which are found in the Kama Sutra *text. Here the couple enjoy themselves in 'the twining position'.*

The Yawning Position

Men seem to have a strong penchant for the yawning position, and your partner is likely to initiate it by lifting your legs on to his shoulders. He can then bear down into you. Movement for you in this position is restricted, and while you may enjoy its flavour of masculine dominance, and love the dynamic feeling of the penis hammering into your vagina, do not let your lover continue for too long in this manner at the expense of you feeling awkward, uncomfortable or sexually remote from what is happening.

Alternate Yawning Position

You may want to vary this position to make it more satisfying and easy for you. Keep one leg rested against his shoulder and lay the other across his thigh. This has the extra advantage of bringing his pubic bone in closer proximity to your vulva, and giving your clitoris vital stimulation.

Pressed and Half-pressed Position

The Pressed Position, described more fully in Chapter Two, suits lovers when the man's *lingam* is of a smaller dimension, but is also an exciting variation to try because it narrows your vagina to create greater friction. If your partner is of aver-

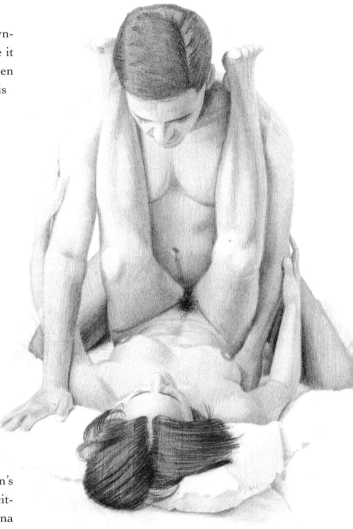

Opposite: the erotic Hindu art on the opposite page shows lovers participating in 'the yawning position'.

Above: many men enjoy the 'yawning position', in which they can bear down on their partners.

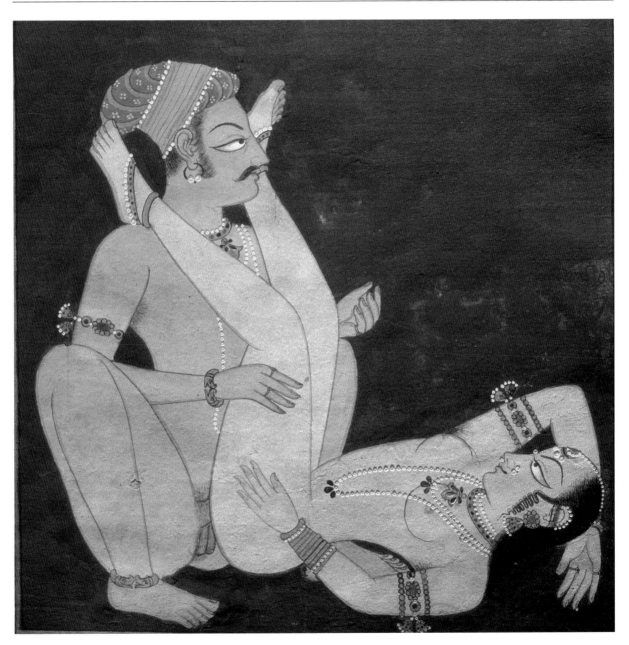

age or large genital size, then he must thrust carefully and with awareness so as not to collide with your cervix. He, of course, needs to be flexible in his pelvis if he is to execute his thrusting rhythmically, especially since he cannot rely on his arms or legs to support his weight and movements.

A more comfortable alternative to the Pressed Position is the Half-pressed Position. Here one leg is stretched out by your partner's side while the other rests on his chest. Like this, your partner's thrusting is more likely to rub against your vulva, arousing you to orgasm.

Blow of the Boar

This position is an erotic variation to add to your repertoire. Here your partner penetrates you from an angle, moving in from the side

and behind your raised thigh as you tilt your pelvis sideways and crook a leg around the back of his body. His movements will excitingly put extra pressure on to your thigh and vulva. In addition, his thrusting will cause his *lingam* to rub against one side of your vagina, thus accomplishing an action of male thrusting which the *Kama Sutra* describes as the 'blow of the boar'.

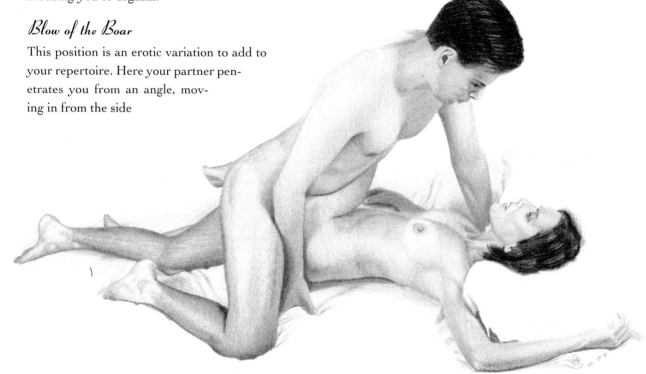

Yoni Power

Yoni power happens when you learn how to control and pulsate your vaginal muscles so that they can tighten around your man's *lingam* and hold it inside you. The *Kama Sutra* calls this lovemaking art the Mare's Position and says that it is learned only by practice (see pelvic floor exercises, Chapter One). Not only will this practise keep you toned and healthy in your genital and reproductive area, it will ensure that you have a happy man indeed! By using these squeeze-release motions, you can hug his *lingam* inside your *yoni* without expending any energy on other movements. It will give you a real sense of sexual power even when your partner is making love to you in the superior position which may otherwise practically immobilize your own pelvis. The contractions within your vaginal cavity will feel to him as if you are milking his *lingam* and drawing it deeper inside of you. A faint-hearted man might even fear that you are going to engulf him! These *yoni* contractions also help you to snugly encompass a man of smaller dimensions than you, and that should guarantee you both satisfaction.

When lovemaking falls into moments of stillness and intimate connection, such as is possible in the Clasping and Twining positions, these subtle contractions within your *yoni* may be all that is needed to keep the penis sufficiently erect while the two of you breathe together, caress, and keep eye contact with each other during moments of harmonious union.

Skills of thrusting

The *Kama Sutra* suggests nine actions of lovemaking that a man can carry out with his female partner. A good lover is a man who can constantly surprise and thrill the woman with a variety of movements during lovemaking so that he can tease all manner of erotic responses from her. A man who establishes a set pattern of thrusting for the duration of intercourse has little imagination, and even less understanding of what excites his partner. Monotonous motion like this is guaranteed to send a woman off into thoughts of her own, so that her mind wanders away from the sexual action and she may secretly wish for him to ejaculate quickly and complete his task. A sensual lover knows that if his thrusting plays between soft and hard, slow and fast, and caresses all sides of her *yoni*, he will exact from his partner the full extent of her ecstasy.

To please his partner sexually, the man needs to relax into lovemaking. He should maintain a constant conscious connection with his woman both emotionally and physically, being inspired by her responses, which he can detect by her breathing, her movements and sounds. Even as he is thrusting, he should caress her whole body, and assure her with his eyes, touches and words that it is to her he is making love, and that he has not become lost in

The Kama Sutra *instructs men on how to vary their thrusting movements. While performing 'the blow of the boar', a man enters the woman from an angled position.*

an agenda of his own. To move rhythmically and fluidly, he should breathe deeply and let his pelvis move, not only back and forth in a rocking motion, but in circles and subtle gyrations. His *lingam* should explore every inch of her *yoni*, seeking out its sensitive and erogenous spots, and it should also stroke her clitoris, the lips of her vulva and her perineum. He should make love to her not only with his *lingam*, but with the whole of his body.

Above: women are urged by the Kama Sutra *to learn the arts of lovemaking by gaining control over their pelvic muscles.*

Right: a woman will be delighted and excited by her lover if he knows how to move rhythmically and vary his thrusting movements during their lovemaking sessions.

These are the nine movements of thrusting suggested by the *Kama Sutra*

"Moving forward"

This is when the vagina and penis unite, and penetration occurs directly.

"Friction or churning"

When the man holds his penis in his hand and churns it around the vagina.

"Piercing"

When the penis pierces downwards into the vagina so that it rubs against the clitoris.

"Rubbing"

When the penis rubs against the lower side of the vagina, particularly if the vulva is raised slightly.

"Pressing"

When the man presses his penis firmly and directly against the vagina.

"Giving a blow"

When the male lover removes his penis from the vagina and then strikes it hard against the vulva.

"The blow of a boar"

When the penis is angled to create friction against only one side of the vagina.

"The blow of the bull"

When the man rubs his penis first against one side of the vagina and then the other.

"The sporting of a sparrow"

This refers to the rapid movements of the penis within the vagina prior to the man's ejaculatory phase.

On the Woman Acting the Part of a Man

Though a woman is usually reserved and keeps her feeling concealed, when she gets on top of a man, she then shows all her love and desire. A man should gather from her actions what her mood is and how she wants to make love.

When a woman has confidence in herself sexually, she is able to take the lead in lovemaking. She can become very creative in her sexual repertoire and make love with all the subtlety and passion of a musician playing on his beloved instrument. When a woman's sexual energy is flowing freely, the body of her lover becomes her lyre, her harp, her cello — and, like the musician, she becomes one with it. The movements, sights, caresses and tempo of her lovemaking may be as sweet and soft as any *dolcetto* tones, or as strong, powerful and strident as the

Known as 'the top', this sexual act requires the woman to be acrobatic and spin herself around on her man.

Right: this 16th-century statue of the great Hindu goddess Kali, known for her sexual prowess, shows her in full fearsome glory.

crescendo of a symphony. She will move harmoniously between the two. When the woman feels sexually uninhibited, she has an unlimited capacity for sexual ecstasy. If she is sensitive to her lover's needs, she will take him with her on her journey of joy.

Kali energy

The *Kama Sutra*, while focusing predominantly on male sexual behaviour, recognizes this aspect of female sexuality. It refers to it as "a woman acting the part of a man," as if it cannot quite bring itself to acknowledge that the intensity of a woman's sexuality is innate to her femininity. The *Kama Sutra*, however, does accept that a woman becomes increasingly sexually uninhibited when she assumes the more assertive "on top" position.

The Hindu Tantric texts, which are more concerned with the spiritual nature of female sexuality

Left: when a woman assumes the superior position during intercourse, she has greater freedom to express her sexual passions.

and less with social etiquette, refer to the female superior sexual position as the "Kali" posture. Kali, the goddess of death and destruction and consort to the god Siva, is much revered throughout India. In the eternal cycle of life, death and rebirth, she is also seen to be the initiator of creation. She is to be feared and loved; she is powerful, compassionate and, simultaneously, terrifying. Her sexual prowess knows no bounds. When Kali makes love to her husband, the mighty and omnipresent Siva, she renders him inert and corpse-like; when she makes love to him, the earth trembles.

Expressing assertiveness

Women should become less afraid of their sexual intensity and learn how to express it joyfully, sensually and orgasmically. A woman can integrate the Kali aspect of herself with the softer and more passive side of her nature. In fact, the *Kama Sutra* urges women to bear in mind the male's traditional role in bed, and to remember that a man needs to know that he is indeed the man in a sexual situation – a coy reminder to the woman to manifest her bashfulness occasionally when she is in the dominant sexual position. Actually, this play between the assertive and passive sides of a woman's sexuality can be a powerful arousal for a man. The *Kama Sutra* suggests that a woman should assume the on-top posture when her lover becomes fatigued during intercourse. This is an excellent idea because it retains the spontaneity in a lovemaking session, and helps the couple to avoid falling into the repetitive movements that occur once the initial sexual enthusiasm

has fallen into a particular pattern. Changing sexual roles also means that the power shifts effortlessly back and forth between the man and woman so that the sexual energy becomes balanced and harmonious. In this way, both partners are able to integrate their own inner male and female energies.

Taking charge

If your man feels secure in his own masculinity he will welcome those occasions when you take charge of the lovemaking and assume the dominant and on-top sexual position. It allows him respite from the constant need to "perform" in bed, which is as burdensome a conditioning as the traditional expectation of submissiveness from a woman. An added bonus is that he is more able to relax, and is thus less likely to ejaculate prematurely. Nevertheless, you must remain sensitive to your lover's level of arousal and take care not to overexcite him before either partner is ready to climax.

In the supine position, your partner is able to lie back and visually enjoy the sensuality of your body as you express yourself sexually. He can touch and kiss your breasts, stroke your belly, and kiss your face as you lower it towards him. He can even increase your excitement by manually stimulating your clitoris.

Freedom of movement

The superior posture has many benefits for you too. Kneeling or sitting astride your love, you can move your whole body freely and without restriction. You are able to position your vulva and undulate your pelvis in ways that maximize clitoral stimulation against your partner's pubic bone. For many women, this clitoral stimulation is an essential factor to achieving an orgasm. The superior sexual position also allows you to control the depth of penetration of the man's penis into your vagina and the pace and tempo of his thrusts. You can play with your lover's arousal, clasping the glans of his penis between the lips of your vagina, and then gently move up and down on it to milk it teasingly. You can sink slowly down on to the shaft of his penis so it fully penetrates your warm depths, freely gyrate your hips so that your partner's member rubs and stimulates all sides of your vagina, or lean backwards so that it presses against the vagina's highly erogenous anterior wall or, possibly, your G-spot. You can let the penis lie outside your vagina and rub your moist vulva over it, which will pleasure both yourself and your lover.

It is essential for you to remain sensitive to your man's penis at all times. You should lower yourself care-

fully on to it and move with awareness, or you may bend it painfully. Keeping eye and verbal contact will ensure that you do not lose touch with each other's physical, sexual, and emotional needs.

Vary the motions

The *Kama Sutra* suggests that when you take the superior position in lovemaking, you may return all the movements suggested for a

Turning like a top, the woman exposes her rear in a sexually provocative and arousing gesture.

137

man in the previous paragraphs. The text recommends three special sexual positions, described below, that the woman can assume in her active role, though the latter two should be taken with a pinch of salt – or undertaken only by the most agile and yogic of readers. The *Kama Sutra* does admit that these positions are only gained by practice.

The Pair of Tongs

To do this, the woman holds the man's penis in her vagina and "milks" it by contracting her pelvic floor muscles. This technique can be extremely arousing for the man because he can feel the vagina's warm, soft walls enfold and release his penis while he remains motionless.

The Top

Here the woman is required to turn around on the man's body like a wheel so that her back is towards him while all the time remaining in sexual contact.

The Swing

The *Kama Sutra* suggests that the man should lift up the middle area of his body so that he elevates himself with his arms and legs, and then the woman rotates her body as in the previous posture. This is an extremely complicated manoeuver, and could put a lot of strain on the man's back.

Whole-body lovemaking

In the superior position, you can use your whole

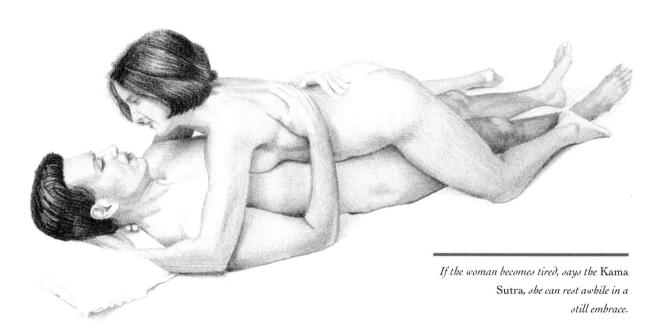

If the woman becomes tired, says the Kama Sutra, *she can rest awhile in a still embrace.*

body to make love. You can lean over your lover and trail your hair and breasts on his skin; or gently kiss his face and neck. You can run your tongue into the folds of his ears and nibble or suck on his nipples – all of which are highly erogenous zones in men. You can use the superior position to experiment with some exciting themes of domination and submission in a playful and harmless way. Ask your partner to stretch his arms out above his head and, leaning over him, pin his hands down with the weight of your own. From here, you can kiss him, tease him, lick, nibble and tantalize him.

Melting together

The *Kama Sutra* advises that when you feel tired in the active role, you can simply lie down on top of your lover and rest without breaking coital contact. You can embrace each other in the Clasping Position (see page 123) and make intimate eye contact and breathe together. There is no reason for either of you to try to hurry things, or move towards a rushed climax. In these soft and tender moments, your bodies can be still, as if melting into one another.

If the penis begins to lose its erection, you have only to move your pelvis gently to restimulate it. Naturally and spontaneously, the sexual energy is bound to arise again and take you both on to another wave of joy. If you prefer, you can resume the supine position and your man can once more take charge of lovemaking, or you may prefer to continue to lead the way. You should always have the choice to surrender yourself to the sweetness of your lover's passion, or to express yourself powerfully and orgasmically.

Sounds of lovemaking

Words which have meanings, and express desire, pleasure, pain and praise, to which may be added sounds like those of the dove, the cuckoo, the green pigeon, the parrot, the bee, the sparrow, the flamingo, the duck and the quail, are all occasionally made use of.

Lovemaking does not have to be a silent affair. In fact, if you have the ability to cast aside inhibitions and allow yourself to express your sexual pleasure through sounds, you can increase the potency of your orgasmic ecstasy.

The sounds that you make may be as soft as a sigh, as gentle as cooing, as haunting as a banshee's wail, or as piercing as screams. Expressing your sexuality through a variety of sounds will bring an aliveness and vitality to your whole body because it deepens your breathing and releases emotional tensions. Tantra teaches that the vibrations of certain sounds stimulates the energy centres of the body (also known as chakras) and awakens the *Kundalini*, the powerful sexual and psychic force which normally lies dormant in the body. This powerful unleashing of energy enables orgasmic feelings to pulsate through your entire body, rather than remaining locked up in the genital area.

The sounds that you make and the words you utter during lovemaking should well up from the

instinctive feelings surfacing within you. Do not force the sounds, but let them be true expressions of the sensation you are encountering emotionally and physically. By bringing your consciousness to those feelings, and expressing them through sound, you are focusing your mind on to the moment-to-moment experience of your lovemaking. In doing this, unexpected things can happen. You may start laughing or crying, and this sexually emotional catharsis can make you feel extremely open and liberated.

If your lover is unafraid of your sexual intensity, he will welcome these audible expressions of your pleasure; they will be an affirmation to him that the lovemaking touches you to the core. Try to encourage him also to freely express his feelings through sounds and words, though at first he may be more inhibited than you are. When a man falls into a monotonous routine of movements and thrusting, he tends to make grunting noises. Exploring his range of sounds will free him from his established pattern of lovemaking and inspire him to become more spontaneous and responsive.

The acknowledgement of the sexual prowess of women is illustrated throughout Hindu art. In this ivory panel carving, the woman assumes the superior position to her yielding male.

CHAPTER SIX

Erotic Acts

"A creative person will multiply
the types of union after the fashion
of the different kinds of animals and birds.
For these variations, performed
according to the preference of each
individual, generate love, friendship
and respect in the hearts
of women. "

Most sexual relationships begin with the flame of passion, and during that period of romance lovers cannot imagine that the fire will burn out. Making love is central to them and probably takes priority over other forms of their communication. New lovers are hungry for each other, ready to explore and experiment with each other's bodies, and eager to know one another as intimately as possible. Something of that first rush of desire should always be kept alive if the relationship is not to succumb to sexually monotonous routines which lack spontaneity and fun. Probably, like most women, you want your sexual life to predominantly express tenderness and sensuality, but it will be to your advantage to make it remain spicy and saucy too. Create time to make love, no mater what other demands encroach upon your time. Show your man that you continue to desire him by allowing impromptu sex to happen. Liberate your love life from the bedroom and nighttime activity and enjoy it sometimes in unusual locations and at unlikely times.

The *Kama Sutra* clearly differentiates between the sexual roles of a courtesan and a wife, though it shows respect to each. Be both to your man so he is continually surprised and delighted by you.

Standing positions

There is something exciting about making love in standing positions, some of which are described in the *Kama Sutra*, because by their nature they imply impromptu sex, hastened by a rush of passion. Sex while standing indicates mutual lust with no time to waste – an urgent desire that demands immediate attention. It does not require the formalities of a bedroom, but can be done against the support of a wall, a door, or even a tree.

The erotic temple sculptures and paintings of India frequently depict couples making love in the standing position, which suggests that this posture was part of the Tantric sexo-yogic tradition and was used by a man and woman during *Kundalini* yoga sexual practices (see Chapter 7).

Supported Congress

If you are approximately the same height as your partner, standing intercourse can be performed by the man penetrating you while you lean against him or something supportive. To do this, though, he probably will have to bend his knees to enter your successfully, turning the act into a veritable "knee trembler." Don't expect too much sensuality while this is going on. A possibly more comfortable way of achieving a similar standing sex act, and one that might be even more exciting, is for you to face the wall and use your hands to lean your weight against it. Your lover can then enter you from a rear position, and you can stand on your toes to gain extra height if necessary. In this position, your lover can further arouse you by manually stimulating your clitoris or caressing your breasts.

The erotic carvings that adorn the walls of the Khajaraho temple in India are a visual monument to the many variations of carnal embrace found in human sexuality.

Suspended Congress

Here the man leans against a wall and supports the weight of the woman by locking his hands together underneath her bottom while she entwines her legs around his waist. She can then do the moving by pressing her feet against the wall to lever herself up and down. This allows the woman to be more active than the previous position and is therefore likely to be more satisfying to her. It does, however, require the woman to be of a lighter weight than the man if he is to lift her with ease. A woman who is too self-conscious about her weight may find it difficult to abandon herself completely to this sexual activity. If your lover is comfortable holding you in this way, try to banish this concern and just enjoy yourself.

Union of the beast and birds

The man and woman can carry out intercourse in the manner of a dog, a goat, a deer, the ass, the cat, the leap of a tiger, the pressing of an elephant and the rubbing of a boar, in addition to the mounting of the horse.

The main differences between how we make love compared to the sexual act of other animals are the choice of positions we adopt and the range and depth of emotions which we apply to sex. The *Kama Sutra*, however, strongly suggests that we should also learn from animal copulation, urging us

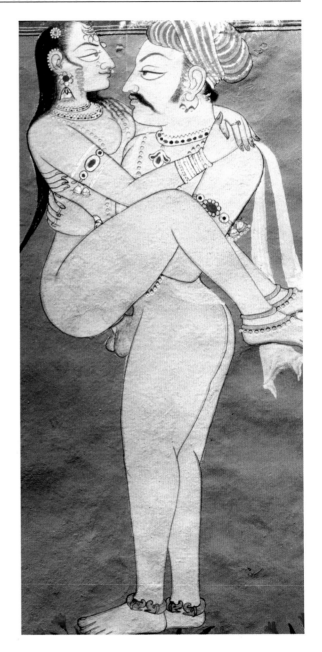

Some of the Kama Sutra *sexual positions require an athletic approach to lovemaking. The standing posture, known as 'suspended congress', is illustrated in this Tantric painting.*

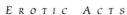

not to be afraid of copying some of their techniques. This, no doubt, will add spice and diversity to your love life, as well as a somewhat bestial sense of naughtiness. Playing at "animals" is fun, and an excellent way to shed inhibitions. Rubbing naked bodies together, nuzzling, rolling around, and imitating the sounds of various beasts in the full thrust of lust is a great way to bring humour into your sex life. Here are one suggestion from the *Kama Sutra* on how to imitate the love antics of a different species.

The Congress of a Cow

Making love "in the manner of an animal" basically refers to rear entry sex, when your partner penetrates your vagina from behind. To achieve this, says the *Kama Sutra*, the woman can support herself on her hands and feet while her partner mounts her "like a bull." You would probably prefer to position yourself more comfortably, such as kneeling on the bed with your rear up and your head lowered towards the mattress. Kneeling beside the bed and laying your top

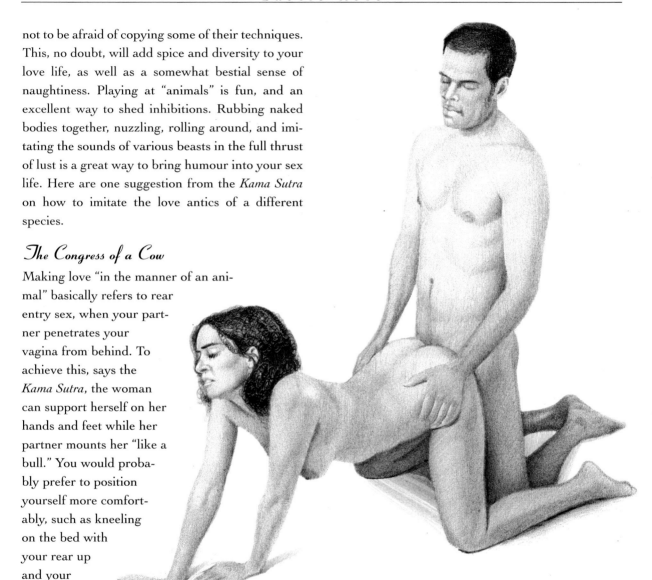

Making love in the fashion of animals (here in the 'Congress of a Cow') is actively encouraged in the texts of the **Kama Sutra**.

half across it for support, with your partner kneeling behind you, also works well. You will be more relaxed if you place a pillow under your stomach and chest so you don't feel as if you are being ground into the mattress.

Some women dislike this rear-entry position because they are embarrassed about showing their backside so prominently, but such a view is very arousing to many men. There is an element of passive surrender in this position for the woman, which might not appeal to you if you are very sexually assertive. On the other hand, the sense of domination can provide a strong turn-on. Your vulva is open and exposed, making penetration easy and potentially deep. Make sure your partner is aware of this, and does not become so carried away with his thrusting that he hurts you. This is not an intimate or cosy position, because your back is turned to your lover, but it is very sexy. Your man can caress your back and hair as he makes love to you. If you elevate your upper body while he is inside you, he can then reach around to stroke your breasts and to rub your clitoris, which would otherwise remain unstimulated. You can also touch your own clitoris to add to your arousal. Rear-entry sex is probably more satisfying to you if you are already high aroused, or if it is only one of a whole variety of positions being played out during intercourse.

> **In all things connected with love, everybody should act according to his or her own inclination.**

Auparishtaka — oral pleasures

While some of the holy scriptures of India condemned oral sex as unclean, the Tantric tradition taught that the woman's *yoni* was a sacred gateway to sexual and spiritual ecstasy, and that her vaginal secretions were like nectar to be supped by the man as the elixir of life; in some parts of India, ancient temples dedicated to the phallic god Siva contain sculptures depicting *Auparishtaka*. Tantra taught that the mixing of the bodily juices and saliva brought balance and harmony between the polar forces of male and female energies. The stance taken by the *Kama Sutra* is that even if something is considered unclean there are times when it is not unclean, and that when two people have oral sex in the context of a loving relationship it is an acceptable practice.

Oral sex is defined as mouth-to-genital contact for the purpose of sexual arousal. When a woman performs it on her man, it is known as fellatio; when a man uses his mouth and tongue to stimulate his lover's vulva it is called cunnilingus. Incidentally, "blow-job", the slang term for fellatio, is misleading since blowing down into your lover's penis is dan-

This Tantric album painting celebrates the erotic pleasures of oral sex. It illustrates 'the congress of the crow', where both partners simultaneously perform the sexual act.

gerous. This caution also applies to air being blown into the woman's vagina.

The public acceptability of oral sex has always fluctuated depending on the culture and era. While the practice of "mouth congress," as it is described in the *Kama Sutra*, is well documented in the arts, sculptures and texts of ancient Eastern traditions, it was a taboo subject in the West until the advent of greater sexual openness in the 1960s. Even the *Kama Sutra* is uncharacteristically conservative about the subject. It describes the practice of fellatio in some detail, but refers to it as an activity performed by eunuchs, or "wanton" women on their male clients during sessions of massage.

Oral sex promotes variety and pleasure in lovemaking when it is performed willingly in an atmosphere of intimacy and trust. It can be a complete sexual episode enjoyed for its own merits, with one lover orally stimulating the other to orgasm, or it may be part of foreplay, used to increase arousal before the act of penetration. Lovers can take turns to kiss and lick each other's genitals, or they may indulge in a mutual act of oral sex, known in the West as '69' and in the *Kama Sutra* as "the congress of the crow."

The Kama Sutra *instructs women on the right techniques of fellatio, exotically entitled 'sucking a mango fruit', so that they should know how to please men.*

Sucking a Mango Fruit

A wise woman who wishes to please her man in bed, and who has no moral objections to mouth congress, should perfect her technique of fellatio. She will know that of all the 64 arts of lovemaking detailed in the *Kama Sutra*, this sexual act is most likely to enchant, excite and capture his heart and imagination.

When a woman, taking her lover's male member into her hand, cherishes it with kisses, caresses it with her tongue, and embraces it with her lips and mouth, she is demonstrating not only her skills of lovemaking, but also her love for her man. Yet a woman must know that she should perform oral sex only when she is willing to do so, when she is comfortable with the intimacy of the situation, and when pleasuring her partner is of paramount importance to her. Then she can do it with a feeling of deep respect for the phallus of her lover. She should regard his member as the embodiment of his sacred masculinity, and kneel before it as the Tantric devotee offers worship to the *lingam* of the god Shiva.

In the *Kama Sutra*, eight acts of fellatio are described as follows.

"The nominal congress"
Hold his member in your hand and, encircling your lips around it, draw your mouth up and down its shaft

"Biting the sides"
Cover the tip of the penis with your fingers "collected together like the bud of a plant" and press the sides of the tip (the glans) with your lips. The *Kama Sutra* suggests also pressing gently with the teeth – but proceed only with extreme caution!

"Pressing outside"
Encircle the end of the penis with your lips and press on it with a sucking motion.

"Inside pressing"
Take the penis deeper into your mouth, pressing it with your lips before taking it out.

"Pressing"
Hold the lingam in your hand and kiss it all over as if you were "kissing the lower lip." In other words, kiss and lick it playfully and sensually.

"Rubbing"
Use your tongue to lick and swirl around the erotogenically sensitive glans.

"Sucking a mango fruit"
Place the penis halfway into your mouth and suck on it firmly, as if drawing the juice out of it.

"Swallowing up"
Take the penis as deeply into your mouth as feels comfortable, pressing firmly on it with mouth and tongue as if you are ready to swallow it up.

Driving him wild

Discover the secrets of your man's desires! Ask him to show you with sounds, sighs, words and grunts of pleasure when you have got the pressure and pace right. Begin oral sex by nuzzling, kissing and caressing his genital area, including the scrotum. Stroke between the folds of his buttocks, and massage his perineum and around his anus with your fingers. As his penis swells, clasp it in one hand and run your tongue all around its highly erotogenic head. Focus your tongue on the sensitive spot (the frenulum) just under the rim of the glans on the underside of the shaft. Don't overstimulate him too quickly but rather turn this act into a tantalizing, long-lasting affair. As you enclose your lips around his penis, relax your jaw and cover your teeth with your lips to avoid hurting him. To control his movements and any sudden thrusts in your mouth, circle your thumb and fingers around the penis to form an extension to your mouth.

Pleasing him

Press firmly with your mouth, tongue, or fingers as you stroke up and down his penis, because most men prefer strong friction. Saying "Does this feel good?" or "Tell me what pleases you," in sultry tones can itself be a major turn-on. Remove his penis from your mouth when you need to relax, but continue the stimulation with your fingers or rub your body and your breasts against his member. Win his heart by telling him, sincerely, how much you appreciate this part of him.

The faster the pace of the stimulation, the quicker your lover will ejaculate. Be alert to signs that he is ready to climax. Some women are ready to accept their lover's seminal fluid into their mouths while others cannot bear the idea of swallowing it, in which case discreet disposal of the body fluid into some handy tissues nearby is the answer. Swallowing the semen is an act of love, done by a woman consciously, and entirely of her own free will and preference. It is a special experience, symbolizing the absorption of her lover and the vitality of his seed into herself and through this act of communion she demonstrates how completely she accepts him.

If you are not prepared to let him ejaculate into your mouth, turn the act of fellatio into intercourse before he reaches the point of no return. Climb astride him and slip his erect penis carefully inside you, or lie down at his side so that he can assume the active role. Alternatively, you can use your hand to stimulate him in the final stages of ejaculation. Letting him ejaculate on your body, belly, or breasts is also very erotic.

Wanton woman

If your lover is thrilled by your "wantonness," become inventive with the mouth congress. Save

This 18th-century Hindu painting shows that a woman, skilled in the arts of love, will know how to caress her partner's lingam in the manner that satisfies him.

it for high days and holidays as a special treat. Take it out of the bedroom routine and surprise him with it in another location when you are sure you are alone. For example, if he is sitting in an armchair, sit on his lap and stroke and kiss him. When he becomes aroused, slide down between his knees and loosen his clothing. Take his member into your hand and caress it until it is fully erect and then perform fellatio on him.

Ask him to allow you to tie his hands with a silk scarf to the top of the bed or another stable object so his arms are held behind his head. Play out a gentle bondage scene with him. Arouse, tantalize and tease him with kisses over his whole body, culminating in an act of fellatio. Kiss, lick and suck him, but move away just before he reaches the ejaculatory stage, continuing to titillate him in other ways. Always return to the mouth congress and when he is nearly crazy and ready to explode, you can take him totally.

Overcoming inhibitions

You may have inhibitions about oral sex. If these objections are of a moral nature, explain this to your partner and ask him to accept your boundaries in the bedroom. You may be concerned about hygiene, but as long as there is no infection present, and your lover has bathed well before lovemaking, his genitals should be perfectly clean and sweet-smelling. Don't worry that in his excitement he may accidentally urinate in your mouth, as during sexual arousal the opening between his urethral tube and bladder automatically shuts off.

Exploring his genitals

Do you feel intimidated by your lover's penis? Often, the only intimate contact a woman has with a man's penis is when it is erect, hard, and demanding! The time, then, has come to know your man's genitalia for both its vulnerability and its power. Ask your partner to be patient and relaxed as you explore his private area and overcome your reservations about oral sex. He must promise not to demand anything more from you than you are willing to do, and must not, on any account, try to thrust or ejaculate. Begin by touching and caressing his genitals without over-exciting him. Take his scrotum into your hand and gently hold it, feeling the weight and shape of his testicles. Explore the perineum and around his anus with your fingertips. Be tender with these parts. When you are ready, bring your face closer to this area, and just rub your cheeks against it, nuzzling into it. When you are comfortable with this, or perhaps on another occasion, repeat the stroking and fondling and then bring your lips into contact with his intimate area, kissing it all over. Don't overstimulate, but if the penis swells, feel its growing firmness in your hand. Be aware of its movements and changing shape. When you are ready, hold the penis in one hand and use your tongue to lick all over its shaft. Progress through each stage of fellatio as described above only when you feel comfortable with doing so. In this way, you can overcome your fears so that both you and your lover can indulge happily in this deeply sensual act.

Love juices

For the sake of such things, courtesans abandon men possessed of good qualities, liberal and clever, and become attached to lowly persons.

A woman who enjoys oral sex will love the man who is unafraid of her *yoni*, and who understands how to make her happy in this way. Invite the man you love to explore your sacred pleasure garden so that his kisses unlock the gateway to your sexual happiness. If you have a caring lover, he will begin by embracing and caressing your whole body, and speaking to you tenderly. He

A woman will devote herself to the man who performs cunnilingus according to her desires, says the Kama Sutra.

will kiss your mouth and everywhere else on your face, as if he is adoring every feature with his lips. Then his tongue can encircle your nipples, which he will suck just as a baby does its mother's breast. As his mouth explores your body, his kisses, licks, and nibbles will trace the terrain of your belly and move down to your inner thighs. At the same time, his hands will stroke you, so every part of you feels embraced in his love. When he cups your buttocks with the palms of his hands, he will tilt your secret parts towards his willing lips. To begin, let him nuzzle into and softly lick your pubic mound and vulva. Then, using the soft, moist brush of his tongue, he can stroke and unfold the petal-like lips of your vulva to reveal the erotic bud of your clitoris. The experienced lover knows that it is too soon to focus his attention solely on this delicate flower of your sexuality, but he may cherish it with gentle kisses before using his tongue to lick your perineum and to dart it like a *lingam* into the dark mysterious cavern of your vagina. As your juices flow, let him sup on this elixir, burying his face against you so he can taste and smell your musky essence.

Stimulating the clitoris

When you are properly aroused, he can turn his attention to your clitoris, always varying the pressures and rhythms of his tongue as he strokes it from underneath, or flicks it from side to side. He can gently suck this jewel, or run his tongue around its sides. He needs to be aware that his strokes have not become monotonous, irritating or automatic, and he must heed your sighs and sounds and understand what is pleasuring you. Indicate your desire if you want him to take you, in this way, to the peak of your ecstasy. When you are approaching your climax, he should sustain the pressure on your clitoris through your orgasm.

An experienced lover knows that after your orgasm this bud may feel tender and sensitive and that you may wish all stimulation to cease. However, if you want him to continue so that you can attain another orgasm, then ask him to do so. If you want your lover to penetrate you before your climax, take his head into your hands and gently pull him towards you.

Smelling sweetly

If you are healthy and happy, and your lifestyle and diet are balanced, do not be afraid that the taste or smell of your vaginal secretions will be offensive to your lover. In fact, the subliminal odour of your love juices acts as a powerful aphrodisiac, attracting the opposite sex to you. When your sexual arousal is heightened and causes the secretions to increase, their normally fragile perfume becomes stronger and even more alluring. Foods containing spices, garlic and onions can affect the taste and smell your secretions, as can smoking cigarettes and certain contraceptive pills. In the days just before your monthly period, your juices can taste more metallic and your lover may prefer to avoid mouth congress at this time. If you notice an offensive smell coming from your vaginal area you need to check with a doctor, who will examine you to see if you have an infection. A burning or itching sensation, or an unusual dis-

In this miniature Hindu painting a couple rejoice in their sexual union without inhibitions.

charge, may also indicate a medical problem. At times like this, abstain from all oral and genital sex until the problem has been treated. Otherwise, all you need to do is to take care of your daily hygiene, washing your private parts with warm water and soap in the bath or shower. You do not need to douche, nor is it advisable to use deodorants or other unguents which may upset the natural balance of flora in your vagina.

Congress of the Crow

When a man and woman lie down in an inverted order, with the head of the one toward the feet of the other, and carry on this congress, it is called the "congress of a crow."

This sexual feast is indulged in by the man and woman simultaneously, and instead of one partner being passive while the other is active, the woman performs fellatio on her lover at the same time that he does cunnilingus on her. Various inverted positions can be assumed, including one where the woman lies head down over the top of the man's body so that her thighs straddle his head, and her *yoni* is close to his mouth. The disadvantage of this position is that while the woman can take the head of the *lingam* into her mouth, her tongue is unable to stimulate that magic spot underneath the rim of its head. An inverted side-by-side position is probably more comfortable and satisfying, each lover resting his or her head on the partner's inside thigh.

Mutual oral sex is deeply sensual and intimate. Enjoy it as a sex act complete in itself, or as a way of arousing each other before or during lovemaking. The simultaneous activity, however, makes it difficult to relax completely into the pleasurable sensations in the same way you would if you were receiving oral sex in a more passive manner. By its nature, you have to stay aware of what you are doing to your partner. Also, during orgasm, the jaw may temporarily spasm so it is definitely safer for the woman to avoid direct oral contact with the *lingam* during her moments of climax!

Lower Congress — anal sex

The *Kama Sutra* refers to anal sex in a very perfunctory manner, simply stating that the practice, which it calls "lower congress," is performed by some people in the southern parts of the country. This lack of detail no doubt reflects its disapproval of such sexual activity, though some historic erotic Oriental and Asian art clearly acknowledges the existence of this practise. In the teachings of Tantra, anal sex was discouraged because it was believed to cause a reversal in the natural upward flow of energy in the body and therefore undermine the physical and spiritual health of participants in such activities.

Even in today's more sexually permissive times, the concept of anal sex remains anathema to most people. It is usually considered to be a sexual activity of male homosexuals, and is rarely acknowledged openly as a sexual variant engaged in by heterosexual couples. Yet many heterosexual partners have experimented with anal intercourse for a variety of reasons. In poorer or less-educated regions, where knowledge or availability of contraception is scant, it is sometimes used as a way of avoiding pregnancy. For other couples, it is enjoyed as an erotic encounter, with its illicit nature adding to its excitement.

The inverted position of partners, indulging in simultaneous oral sex, is commonly referred to as the '69' position. The Kama Sutra *calls it 'the congress of the crow'.*

Generally, women are less likely than men to approve of anal sex, and they may regard it as an unhygenic, humiliating, and even immoral practice. For most women, the vagina is the natural receptacle of loving sexual relations, designed by nature to embrace the penis during intercourse, and to provide the passage for the fruit of that union in childbirth. A woman may not be able to countenance the idea of anal penetration, her main association with the anus being that of an organ whose structure and function are designed to expel waste matter from the body. Also, anal penetration can be painful for a woman, causing rupture of the blood vessels, unless it is undertaken with great sensitivity by her partner and in a climate of mutual consent.

The thrill of surrender

There may be times when anal sex is acceptable to a woman, and she may even encourage it, but it is unlikely that she will want to participate in it on a frequent basis or for it to be considered a standard part of lovemaking. Those special times may arise from her desire to surrender her body totally and passionately to her lover with no holds barred. On these occasions, the man must be sure that he has her permission and the woman has not been coerced against her true will. The woman should adopt a comfortable position, such as kneeling on the bed with her head lowered, with pillows beneath her to cushion her body. Alternatively, she may prefer to take the superior position so that she is in more control of the depth of penetration. The anal sphincter is naturally tight, and not designed for penetration, so it is best if the man first gently relaxes it by massaging it with his fingers, spreading a lubricant such as KY Jelly around its rim and interior with his fingers. He should then penetrate her very slowly and gently, continuing onwards only with her permission. If she is experiencing pain or fear, he should stop immediately, and on no account must he thrust deeply or unexpectedly unless she wills him to do so. If the woman is happy to experiment with penetrative anal sex, she can increase her pleasure by manually stimulating her clitoris at the same time.

If penetrative anal sex is unacceptable to either partner the woman can still derive pleasure from anal stimulation, allowing her lover to massage and finger pressure the rim of this erogenous zone while making love in the normal way.

Anal hygiene

Good hygiene is of paramount importance if anal sex is to take place. The rectum is a repository of natural bacterial matter, and care must be taken that this is not transferred to the vagina or it may instigate a serious pelvic infection. Ideally, the man should use a lubricated condom during anal penetration. However, many makes of condoms are designed for vaginal use only, and tend to rip easily in the tighter confines of the rectum. Certain brands of condoms, designed for male homosexual penetrative activity, are therefore more suitable. After anal sex, the man should always thoroughly cleanse his penis before any vaginal intercourse takes place.

HIV, hepatitis B and other sexually transmitted diseases are spread more easily via anal sex because the friction is more likely to break the rectum's membranes and cause body fluid to blood contact. Therefore, anal sex must never be part of your sexual repertoire unless you are absolutely sure of each other's sexual history and health status. It is not something you should ever participate in during a casual sexual encounter.

Arousing him anally

You can help your man experience a different and more heightened level of orgasmic arousal by using your fingers gently to stimulate his anal area and prostate gland. One of the functions of the prostate gland, which is located behind the front wall of the man's rectum and just below his bladder, is to produce the seminal fluid which is secreted during ejaculation. Pressure on this walnut-sized gland during the peak of sexual arousal can enhance and prolong your man's orgasmic reflexes. Take time together to explore this hidden erogenous area of his body. You may both feel more comfortable if he douches his rectum prior to this experiment, or you may decide to wear thin surgical gloves. If you are using your fingers without protection, ensure that your hands are clean and your nails are short and smooth. Always wash your hands thoroughly afterwards.

This painting illustrates a sexual act where the man penetrates the woman's vagina from the rear position in the manner of an animal.

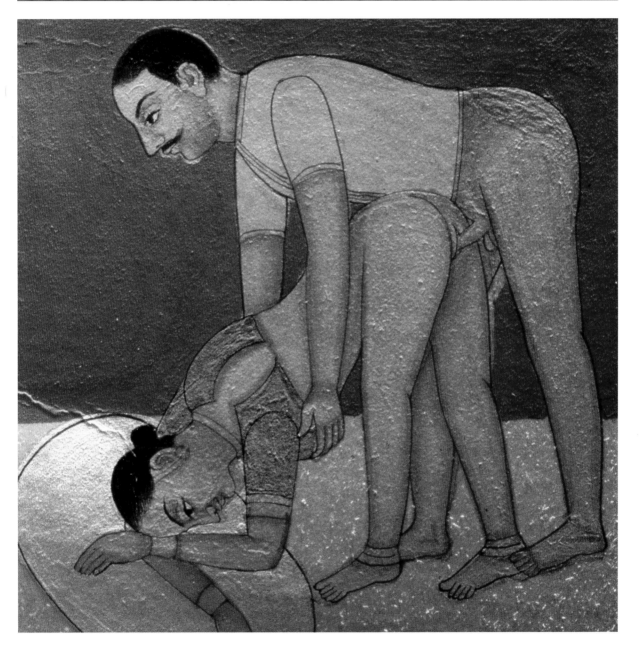

Apply a little lubricant such as KY Jelly to the anal orifice and press gently all around its surface with your fingertips. Take your time, so that your partner can start relaxing this sphincter muscle. Encourage him by suggesting that he breathes deeply down into his belly and towards his anus. Ask him to visualize the outgoing breath as rendering this area softer and more open. After a while, slip a fingertip just a little way inside his rectum and press steadily and rhythmically all around its walls, delving a little higher as he continues to relax. Now focus your finger pressure towards the front wall closest to his genitals, and probe gently until you feel the firm bulk that is the prostate gland. Pressing or rubbing your finger against this highly erogenous spot may induce intensely pleasurable and erotic sensations, possibly leading to orgasm.

Between pleasure and pain

Regarding sexual activity, there can be no definite rules. Once lovemaking has begun, passion gives birth to all manner of acts of the parties involved.

The *Kama Sutra* is realistic about passion. While it encourages tenderness and skill in lovemaking, it acknowledges that within the energy of sex are untamed forces which, once unleashed, are unpredictable and wild. The book compares those lovers who are blind with passion with the impetuosity and "blind speed" of a horse at full gallop. In the frenzy of passion, a woman can become aggressive in her sexuality and assume the characteristics normally associated with the man. However, says the *Kama*

Sutra, once the passion is spent, these "contrary results" soon revert to normal.

Lovemaking blows

When the senses are inflamed, lovemaking may become a far from gentle activity. It can look as if the lovers are actually fighting each other as they may pummel, strike, bite, scratch and pull each other's hair, though hopefully not in such a manner as to cause unwelcome pain or injury. A battle of domination and submission starts, and at this stage either role may be eagerly adopted by the man or the woman. The *Kama Sutra* lists the head, shoulders, chest, back, abdomen and sides of the body as areas where lovers can aim their playful blows. In addition, it says that striking is of four kinds: striking with the back of the hand, with fingers a little contracted, with the fist and with the flat of the palm. These, however, are not set rules, for, as the *Kama Sutra* admits, rules are the first thing to go in the heat of passion.

Women are bound to view the sado-masochistic element of sex in mixed ways. For some it will be an incomprehensible activity, since what they crave from lovemaking is solely tenderness and intimacy. Others will relish it, and appreciate an opportunity to give vent to their ecstatic but darker sexual desires. As the *Kama Sutra* says, "Such passionate

---

Some women enjoy playing out the darker side of their sexuality with their partners within mutually agreed boundaries.

actions and amorous gesticulations which arise on the spur of the moment and during sexual intercourse, cannot be defined, and are as irregular as dreams."

Sexual fantasies

Bondage, tying each other up, spanking and dressing in outlandish hosiery and leather gear while participating in sexual activity are all possible manifestations of the fertile world of sexual fantasies. There is no harm done by these activities if you are safe in the knowledge that what happens in privacy between you and your lover is borne out of passion, but done in an atmosphere of mutual consent and trust. What is important is that you do not feel coerced into rough play against your will, or damaged by it. The bottom line is that you should be confident of maintaining a control of the situation at all times. Talk over with your partner the issues of rough sex or acting out sexual fantasies and be honest with each other about your desires, inhibitions and boundaries.

Three's a crowd

When a man enjoys two women at the same time, both of whom love him equally, it is called the "united congress." Threesomes and group sex is the stuff of erotic fan-

The Hindu god Krishna is seen in this painting flirting and frolicking by the riverside with the female goat herders, known as 'gopis'.

tasies, and should probably remain as such. While some women may find the idea exciting and arousing in the privacy of their thoughts, the reality is more likely to be debasing and potentially emotionally harmful.

Few women are so emotionally detached from their partners that they happily embrace the idea of sharing them with other people. If you are confronted with a potential sexual episode of this type, and are tempted to try it out, search your soul carefully as to why you want to engage in this experiment. Ask yourself these questions, and be honest with your answers. Are you being coerced into a threesome by an over-eager lover, or a bisexual girlfriend? If this is the case, and you are not one hundred per cent positive about becoming involved, then be strong and dismiss the suggestion. Don't be afraid to appear unadventurous or inhibited! Can you accept seeing your lover pay sexual attention to another woman and not be filled with recrimination and self-doubt afterwards? If the answer is no, then know yourself, and state your case clearly. Do you absolutely know the sexual history and health of the prospective partners? If you are not sure, forget it, unless you all agree to safer sex practices.

If you do want the experience of a threesome, it will be to your advantage if you find the other woman attractive too. Some men fantasize about a threesome not so much because of the extra attention they personally will receive but because they are aroused by seeing two women make love. If this idea turns you on too, then at least you will be equally erotically satisfied by the escapade.

Sex with several partners

The *Kama Sutra* calls sex between one man and many women "the congress of the cows." If the situation is reversed, with one woman and more than one male lover, then no doubt it could be called "the congress of the bulls." The *Kama Sutra* says that this type of sexual activity might take place if a courtesan is alone with many men, or if a man shares his woman with his male friends, so that they all enjoy making love to her at the same time.

The *Kama Sutra* was written at a time when women generally were of low status in society, and were perceived as objects of male pleasure. Sexually active women were usually courtesans, or, in other words, high-class prostitutes. A contemporary woman is unlikely to put herself in such an impersonal and sexually objectified situation, nor would she be wise to do so. Such an escapade is dangerous for a woman because she would have little control over its outcome, and would gain little respect or sympathy from others if things went wrong. More importantly, in an age where both men and women have had to become increasingly aware of the dangers of sexually transmitted diseases, engaging in sex with multiple partners would be dangerous and potentially life-threatening.

Secret fantasies

It is not at all uncommon for a woman to fantasize about making love with many men in a licentious or potentially dangerous situation where she feels out of control. This fantasy may fuel her arousal when she masturbates or even when she makes love to her partner. She may well feel confused as to what these taboo sexual thoughts, which appear to be in direct contrast to her apparent longing for tender, respectful, and sensual lovemaking, say about her deepest desires and sense of self-worth.

The truth is that women often have very fertile imaginations when it comes to sexual fantasises, yet these fantasies almost certainly have nothing to do with their real-life needs and desires. An erotic fantasy may appear to place the woman in a situation of being humiliated, but the reality is that she is always in control of her fantasy because she can shut it off when she wants. It is her creation! It does not represent any true longing to be debased, but acts as a safety valve for the release of the intenser, darker and exciting element of danger which exists within the huge landscapes of human sexuality.

Making love in water

Making love in water was prohibited by religious law in ancient India, and the *Kama Sutra* upheld the view that it was improper behaviour. This disapproval was probably based on the fact that in India many rivers are deemed sacred. Lakes and ponds are communally used by the villages, and the daily ablutions, which are still carried out at water sites, are part of strict religious practice. Whereas we have access to the luxuries of baths, whirlpools and Jacuzzis for recreational use, the water supplies of India were and are precious commodities vital to everyone's life. The *Kama Sutra*, however, does quote one sage, Suvarnanabha, who suggested that lovers should practice complex

sexual positions in water because it allows for ease of movement. In fact, making love in water is wonderful and should be experienced by all lovers in search of the lovemaking arts. Water makes you light and buoyant, taking away your concerns about weight and enabling your body to move gracefully. In particular, the standing postures such as the Suspended and Supported Congress can be elegantly achieved

Making love in the surrounds of nature, or in water, is a joyful experience if privacy can be ensured.

once the problems of gravity are resolved. Water's liquid touch is sensual to your skin, relaxes your mind, and makes your nakedness feel natural.

CHAPTER SEVEN

Transcendental Sexuality

" This work is not intended
to be used merely as an instrument
for satisfying our desire. **"**

*I*t is in the nature of woman to invite the sacred into the sexual act. A woman's whole being longs for union of body, mind, and soul with her beloved. She instinctively knows the transcendental quality of lovemaking, for the essence of her female sexual energy is bliss.

According to Tantra, the ancient spiritual philosophy of India, a woman is the supreme initiator of sacred sexuality. She is a goddess of love, and she is the divine instrument through which basic human sexuality is transformed to a higher state of consciousness.

Tantra, which flourished in India and Tibet from around 5000 years ago, taught that the conscious sexual union of woman with man was a potent force for inner transformation. It is not the only philosophy to venerate sexuality as a sacrament. Similar beliefs were held in Taoist thought in China, and prevailed in ancient Egyptian and Greek rites. It was integral to pagan religions all over the world.

The quest for the transformation of the spirit through the involvement and celebration of the sensual body has recurred at different times and in different cultures throughout history. Central to this is the role of the woman, who is held in the highest esteem, and whose sexuality is honoured as the gateway to transcendence of flesh and spirit.

This view of woman, of course, is in strong contrast to the centuries of orthodox and patriarchal religious conditioning which has taught that a woman is subordinate to a man, and that her sexuality is treacherous to a man's spirituality unless it is controlled. In this system of belief, the body and the spirit are divided as if they were enemies, and the potential for sexual ecstasy is repressed. A woman's true nature cannot be fully acknowledged or respected, for she is cast into either the role of the virtuous Madonna or Eve, the eternal temptress. All philosophies which adhere to the transcendental aspect of sexuality, however, acknowledge the woman in the wholeness of her nature and encourage men to honour the female body and its sexuality.

Concepts of Tantra

While it is not at all necessary to engage in esoteric beliefs or practices to enrich your sexual relationship, it is interesting and inspiring to understand some aspects of the complex ideas which form the basis of Tantric teaching on sexuality. They are, in particular, very empowering for women, and they can help you to view your sexuality in a positive light.

Hindu Tantra teaches that the state of primordial bliss, or cosmic consciousness, is formed from the merging of polar male and female energies into a state of perfect equilibrium. Out of this cosmic union of opposing principles, which can also be described in terms of "active and passive,"

The seven principal energy centres, seen here in the 'subtle body', are called 'chakras'. They are activated by the creative force of vital energy known as the 'Kundalini'.

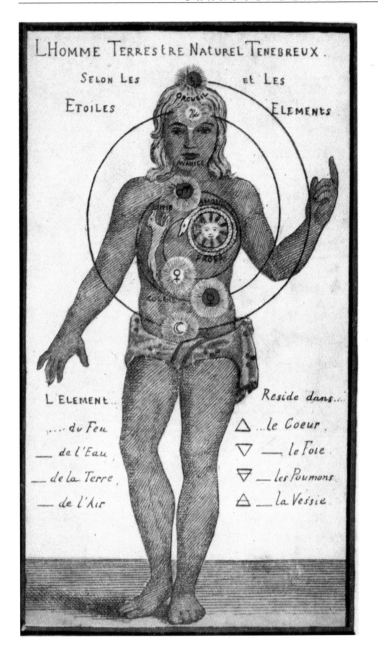

LHomme Terrestre Naturel Tenebreux.

Selon Les   et Les

Etoiles   Elements

L'Element..

....du Feu

___ de l'Eau

___ de la Terre,

___ de l'Air

Reside dans...

△ ..le Coeur

▽ __ le Foie

▽ __ les Poumons

△ __ la Vessie

"positive and negative," and "matter and energy," comes the powerful creative force of nature. Thus, when a man and woman are sexually united and, through their love and awareness, attain a harmonious state of physical and spiritual union, they are enacting the sacred mystery of the divine cosmic principle. In Tantric lovemaking, the man is honoured as a god, and the woman is worshipped as the goddess.

Sexuality, therefore, is one pathway to spiritual realization. The body is its instrument. The five physical senses are not only the means through which to experience bodily pleasure and joy, but are also, as the *Kama Sutra* states, the "windows of the soul"; they are the bridges which link the individual spirit to the existential state of pure consciousness.

The Kundalini

Tantra teaches that within the physical form of every human being exists a correlative etheric body which houses the same potent energy forces which govern the universe, and within this subtle plane there are seven principle energy centres, known as *chakras*. Also within the energy body resides the *Kundalini*, the powerful feminine creative force which is manifested in every aspect of existence. In the normal course of human life, this is likely

Tantric disciples practise meditation, breathing techniques and sexo-yogic postures under the guidance of an enlightened teacher to attain a transcendental state of love and consciousness.

to remain inert. However, according to Tantric thought, the *Kundalini*, depicted in Eastern art as a sleeping serpent coiled three and a half times around upon itself, can be awakened through certain practices and activities, known as *Kundalini-yoga*. These practices are almost always performed under the strict guidance of an enlight-

ened teacher. When the *Kundalini* arises from its dormancy at the base *chakra*, which is located on an etheric level at the base of the spine, it travels up through the energy body, unfolding a higher state of consciousness at each *chakra*.

Ultimately, once the *Kundalini* reaches the supreme *chakra*, which is situated in the 'subtle body' above the crown of the head, this dynamic female energy is reunited with the male principle of pure consciousness. In this merging, the duality of male and female polarities ceases to exist, and a state of cosmic bliss is realized.

Sexual yoga

The *Kama Sutra*'s approach to sexuality is robust, pragmatic and technical, but its uncensored endorsement of sensuality and eroticism clearly has its roots in the Tantric tradition. Although it predominantly addresses men, it never neglects to state the importance of female sexual happiness which is fundamental to the concept of transcendental sexuality.

Many of the sexual positions described in the *Kama Sutra* are complicated and, to the modern mind, would require the skills of an accomplished contortionist. In fact, they have their basis in the *Kundalini-yoga* discipline of Tantric tradition. These sexo-yogic postures were practiced by Tantric disciples during sexual rituals to obtain mastery over body and mind. Together with breathing techniques, and the repetition of certain vibratory sounds, or mantras, and other medita-

tive practices, Tantric adepts used these postures to awaken the *Kundalini* energy. As Tantric sexuality discourages unnecessary wastage of semen, considering it to be a source of vital life energy for the man, many of the sexo-yogic positions enabled the male disciple to gain control over his orgasmic reflexes in order to prevent involuntary ejaculation during copulation. In addition, yoga, which means union, is a discipline which works to integrate body, mind, and spirit, and many *Kundalini-yoga* postures were devised to heal physical, emotional, mental, and sexual conditions.

The *Kama Sutra* text admits readily that many of its sexual positions can be achieved only through long years of practice. While many of the sexual postures already described in this book can be adapted to the satisfaction and comfort of today's lovers, others should be attempted only by people who are experienced in the discipline of *Kundalini-yoga*. If you are agile and loose of limb, some of the more advanced but less-contorted sexual positions may be possible to achieve with considerable practice and lots of humour.

Turning Position

The Turning Position is one example of a sexual position *"learned only by practice."* As the couple are making love, and the man is in the superior posture he is advised to turn his body around without withdrawing his *lingam* from the woman's *yoni*. Once this astonishing feat is accomplished, the woman is then advised to embrace her lover around his back.

Splitting A Bamboo

The *Kama Sutra* describes a position called "Splitting A Bamboo." It is a variant of the Yawning Position, where the woman raises both legs and places her feet on her partner's shoulders. In this advanced position, you place one leg on your lover's shoulder while the other is stretched out on the bed. While making love, you constantly alternate the positions of your legs, raising and stretching out each limb by turn. Concentration is needed to carry out these movements with elegance and ease, and you will have to be flexible in your hips and pelvis. This position presses and rubs your *yoni* against your lover's *lingam*, thus increasing your mutual pleasure.

Sexual movements such as the Yawning Position and Splitting a Bamboo which cause you to raise your legs and open wide your thighs readily expose your vulva during lovemaking. Do not be afraid of this, for Tantra regarded this intimate part of a woman as sacred, and the gateway to all divine sexuality. One Tantric text spoke lovingly of a woman's *yoni* as a "lotus flower, an ocean filled with Bliss."

'Splitting a bamboo' is a tantric sexual position where the woman moves one leg and then the other to her partner's shoulders.

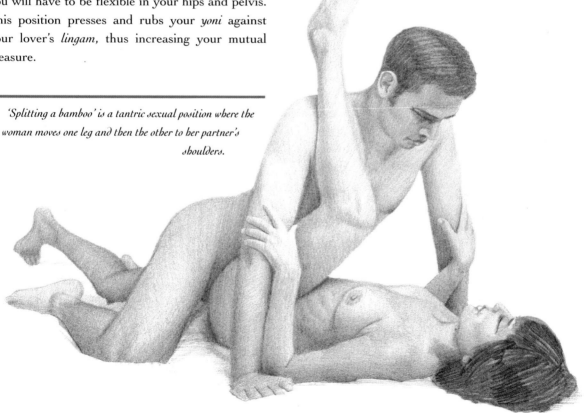

Lotus-like Position

This lovemaking position emulates the basic sitting posture used during the practice of the yogic *pranayama* technique, a meditation exercise which focuses awareness on the breath. The lotus position

The lotus position allows the upward release of Kundalini energy, and the crossed position of the legs creates a sealed circular energy flow within the body.

is commonly used by meditators because the extended spine allows the upwards release of *Kundalini* energy, and the crossed position of the legs creates a sealed circular energy flow within the body.

The "lotus-like" sexual posture requires you to fold your legs one over the other on the level of your abdomen, thus leaving your vagina exposed and tilted to receive your lover's thrusting. Only the most agile of women could accomplish this position or maintain it for any length of time.

Transforming Your Sex Life

It is not necessary to believe in any specific philosophy in order to transform your sexual relationship so that it becomes deeply intimate and emotionally and physically satisfying. You do not have to participate in esoteric practice, nor is it necessary to have a spiritual or cosmic agenda about your sex life. Your purpose of incorporating elements of transcendental lovemaking into your relationship may lie purely in your desire to deepen the love and sexual commitment between you and your partner.

Passionate start

At the beginning of a relationship, you are probably happy to surrender yourself to the passionate nature of your lovemaking. In fact, passion and love are such powerful forces in themselves that they can ignite the transcendental *Kundalini* energy within you. The friction and stimulation of your sex organs, the deeper breathing and sounds that you make, all stimulate the *Kundalini* so that your sex and heart centres are spon-

taneously opened – hence that amazing sense of *oneness* that you feel with a new beloved. In that initial glow, you instinctively see the god and goddess in one another. You feel not only merged with each other, but at one with the whole world. This is the experience of union that is the essence of transcendental sexuality.

However, as time passes, and your relationship becomes more familiar and settled, the passion almost inevitably begins to subside. Your lovemaking may fall into a more routine pattern, losing some of its spontaneity and sparkle. Your personal responsibilities and duties resurface to the forefront of your life to make demands upon your time, and it takes considerable awareness to prevent your sexual relationship from becoming dull and to avoid taking each other for granted, losing the sense of wonder and gratitude that you initially experienced with each other.

Seeking an alternative way

You may feel it is now relevant to find an alternative approach to lovemaking in order to rekindle the tenderness and sensuality of an earlier time – or, perhaps, you and your partner have experimented with many sexual techniques, and while your relationship lacks nothing on the level of physical satisfaction you both yearn to explore a more meaningful dimension of lovemaking. Perhaps you wish to engage in meditative sexuality right at the beginning of a relationship. In any of these circumstances, you will need to have a like-minded partner who is willing to explore the possibilities of transcendental sexuality with you.

The bowed posture assumed by the woman in this Hindu painting will initiate deep breathing and a release of sexual energy.

As a woman, you are likely to find that transcendental lovemaking appeals to your feminine nature and emotional and sexual needs. However, you must be patient with your partner, and encourage him to experiment with these different concepts of making love which may initially go against the grain of his masculine sexual conditioning. Do not abandon all your accustomed patterns of lovemaking in one go, but select times to experiment with a slower and more meditative approach to sex. Be playful with each other in bed as you explore the concepts described below, and do not feel compelled to perform in a prescribed way. Use the ideas which suit you both, and do not impose rules on each other. Do, however, give yourselves time to discover that lovemaking has a depth to it which is absolutely divine.

Honest communication

Transcendental sexuality requires you to be sexually and emotionally honest, keeping open all your lines of communication with one another. Do not allow niggling tensions to build up, but agree to share your thoughts and feelings honestly, albeit without blaming or hurting each other. Respect each other as individuals who have different needs and respond to the other's vulnerabilities. A committed relationship is one where both partners should be able to share their hopes and fears, their strengths and their weaknesses. Listen to each other carefully before interrupting, learning to respect the other's points of view without necessarily taking them on board as your own. If sexual issues are causing you concern, discuss these matters in the spirit of two people mutually committed to the growth and development of your sexual relationship. Do, however, avoid tense discussion of sexual matters at the time when you are

This illustration from a 19th-century palm leaf manuscript shows the couple making love in a spoon-like position with the woman's back moulded into the front of her lover's body.

making love, as this can easily be misunderstood and egos can be hurt. Talk over these matters at a time when you are both relaxed. Phrase what you need to say with tact and love, taking responsibility for your feelings. For example, rather than saying, "You should be doing this . . ." try to rephrase it in a subjective manner, such as, "I would love it if you could do this . . ."

Be meditative

Meditative lovemaking has a stillness in it that is qualitively different than the type of 'bumping and grinding' effort you might associate with hot and lusty sex. Try to bring the essence of meditation into aspects of your life so that it is naturally

implemented into your sexual relationship. Deal with your issues and duties at the appropriate times, and then let go of your anxieties and tensions so that you can relax. Do not carry your worries into your lovemaking. Learn to enjoy silence and non-activity, taking the opportunity when it arises to sit quietly and peacefully. Be aware of the thoughts that pass through your mind, but try not to become over-identified with them.

The key tool of meditation is breath awareness. Practise breathing deeply and slowly, especially in times of crisis, and you will soon see how it helps you to become calmer. Join a meditation class, so that an accomplished teacher can show you some of the breathing and awareness techniques that will help you to develop your own inner centre of peace. Meditate regularly, alone or with your lover, sitting quietly with closed eyes and with minds focused on breathing.

Breathing is the vehicle of vital life energy, and it is the link that connects and integrates body, mind and spirit. When making love, breathing deeply and slowly together opens the heart and feelings, sensitizes and energizes the body, and enhances the mediative quality of your sexual communion.

Total Commitment

To transform your sexual relationship so that it becomes an enduring source of inspiration and joy, you both need to make a total commitment to your lovemaking so that it is absolutely central to your relationship. You must create time to make love, putting it as a priority in your lives, regardless of your other responsibilities. This does not mean, however, that sex should feel like a chore. When you learn to make love in a transcendental way, you will discover that, because of its meditative nature, it does not rob you of energy. As it has no goal, or agenda attached to it, such as the imperative to reach an orgasm, there is no tension in it. The whole premise of transcendental lovemaking is based on honouring and respecting each other. Neither partner should feel that they are being used solely for the purpose of physical gratification.

Daily Communion

Even if you do not have the time, or the desire, to engage in a prolonged period of lovemaking, you can still connect intimately with each other on a daily or regular basis. It is not necessary to be sexually excited or active, nor is it essential for your man to have a full erection. He can enter you even while his penis is still fairly soft and undemanding. Lay together in a quiet embrace, with his *lingam* resting inside your *yoni*. You may want to pulsate your vaginal muscles, to provide a small amount of stimulation so that his *lingam* stays inside of you. Relax your bodies and breathe together, and look into each other's eyes. Or close your eyes and submerge yourselves into this loving and deeply intimate embrace.

Ritualising Lovemaking

By ritualising your lovemaking, you give it a special significance that acknowledges its revered role in your relationship. You can still have spontaneous and lusty sex when you feel like it, but ritual helps to transform the occasion whenever you intend to make love in a transcendental way.

• Take plenty of time to relax with each other before you make love. Let go of mental concerns, focusing your thoughts on each other. Luxuriate in an aromatic bath together and then anoint and massage each other's bodies with lotions and oils to enliven the skin and the senses. You may want to prepare a meal of light and delicious foods, accompanied by a fine wine, which you enjoy together.

• Prepare the bedroom or location where you intend to make love so it becomes a warm, romantic, and welcoming temple dedicated to sensual joy. Bathe the room in candlelight and light an aromaburner to fill it with the exotic fragrance of essential oils which are emotionally relaxing yet sexually stimulating. Clear the room of any clutter that will distract the eye and mind, and decorate the environment with cushions and fabrics that are soft and sensual to the touch and harmonious and inspiring in colour.

Right: prepare the room where you intend to make love with devotion as if you were adorning a temple of worship.

Below: Tantric lovers treasure the still moments of sexual union, taking time to make eye contact and merge together.

• When Tantric lovers engaged in ritual lovemaking, they gave gifts to each other and placed offerings on a shrine to invoke the presence of the sacred god and goddess. You may or may not want to create a spiritual ritual, but a symbolic gesture which honours each other will focus your awareness on the special significance of the event. Perhaps you could create a small altar in one corner of the room by placing a silk cloth of Tantric red colour on a small table or on the floor. When you enter the room with your lover, you could each place a flower on the altar and light two candles dedicated to your love. You can be imaginative with this ritual, creating it according to your own preference. Alternatively, you may simply want to take each other's hands and say, "I love you, I honour you."

Transcendental lovemaking

A person acquainted with true principles of this science, and who preserves his Dharma, Artha, and Kama . . . is sure to obtain the mastery over his senses.

Transcendental sexuality is extremely sensual lovemaking, but though the flame of passion may initially ignite the sexual energy, it is not essential for its continuation. You should try to consciously moderate the impulsiveness of your physical excitement to allow a sustained meditative quality of feeling to exist between you. This type of lovemaking is cool passion rather than hot passion. It does not have an end in sight, so the focus is not on reaching orgasm, even though that may occur at some later stage of intercourse. The purpose is to use your orgasmic energy for transformation of mind and body, rather than dissipating it prematurely through climaxing and bringing your lovemaking to a hasty conclusion.

Slow awakening

Spend a long time on foreplay, kissing and caressing each other with great tenderness. Sensual pleasuring is especially important for the woman, who may need time to become fully ready, both sexually and emotionally, to make love. Your partner will also benefit from this slow sensual awakening, as it will draw his sensations of arousal away from his genital area to flood the whole of his body.

You can both engage in oral sex if you take pleasure in this practice. Honour each other's intimate areas with the presence of your lips and tongue. Your partner can drink the love juices which flow from your *yoni*, for this elixir is deemed, by the teachings of Tantra, to be energy-giving to the man, and to have a harmonizing effect on your mutual energies. You may worship his *lingam* with your lips, but you must take care not to overstimulate your partner to ejaculation because this would be a premature waste of his semen. If by chance he does ejaculate, accept this happening in the spirit of reverence.

Oral sex can be highly arousing for either partner, and it is important during this stage of transcendental lovemaking that you engage in it for sensual and sexual awakening and for honouring the *lingam* and *yoni*, but not to cause over-excitement or orgasm for either of you.

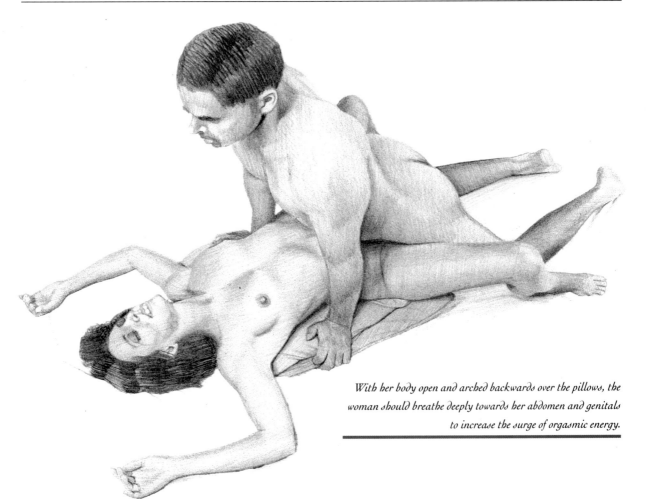

With her body open and arched backwards over the pillows, the woman should breathe deeply towards her abdomen and genitals to increase the surge of orgasmic energy.

Other sexual teachings

The *Kama Sutra* is one of a number of important works on sexual behaviour to have originated in India that prescribes specific lovemaking positions. In the 16th century, a text called the *Ananga Ranga* appeared, which seemed to draw strongly on the teachings of ancient texts, and in particular the *Kama Sutra*. The main difference between these two texts was that the latter book placed sexuality in a more moralistic context, and was directed towards married couples only. Even so, some of its prescribed positions reflected the Tantric origins of transcendental sexual practice.

One example of an *Ananga Ranga* sexual posture has the woman's body arched backward in a bow position. To achieve this, you should lie down on the bed while your partner places several pillows below your buttocks and one beneath your head. This raises up your vulva, while your torso arches back. By directing your breath deep down into your abdomen and towards your exposed and opened genitals, and by expressing your sexuality with signs and moans of pleasure, you may experience a powerful surge of orgasmic energy building up through your whole body.

Another *Ananaga Ranga* position suggests that the man sits with out-stretched legs while the woman lowers herself on to his lap, so that his *lingam* slips into her *yoni*. She then stretches out her legs so that their limbs form the shape of the spokes of a wheel. This position is a perfect one to assume when the sexual energy is high and you wish to remain in the plateau phase of your lovemaking so as not to precipitate an early orgasm. Leaning your bodies slightly backwards, you should visualize that the orgasmic energy is being drawn up through the body towards the crown of your head. Gaze softly into one another's eyes and synchronize your breathing to increase a feeling of energetic merging. Let your hearts be open and vulnerable and in communion.

The couple adopt a sitting position with legs outstretched. They make eye contact and breath harmoniously together as they rock gently back and forth.

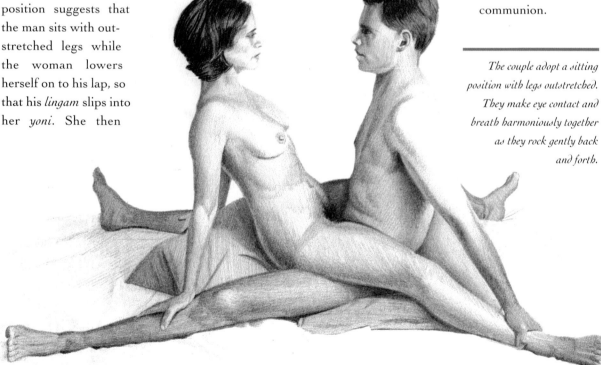

Visualizing the sacred

Transcendental sexuality does not encourage lovers to become lost in erotic fantasy while making love because this can cause them to fall out of harmony with each other. Fantasy can be a useful tool in inciting sexual excitement, and it can help individuals to achieve an orgasm which they might otherwise fail to do. However, if the lovers are caught up in their own mental images in the pursuit of increased sexual arousal, it is difficult to remain in deep communion with each other. Lovemaking then becomes a collision of bodies rather than a merging of hearts and souls.

However, visualization did play a role in ancient Tantric lovemaking rituals because the man and woman would hold an image of the sacred god, or goddess, in their minds as they made love to each other. The woman was perceived as the personification of the goddess Shakti, the feminine principle of cosmic creation, and the man was beheld as the personification of the god Siva, the male principle of cosmic consciousness. Their sexual ritual was an enactment of that eternal dance of cosmic sexual union between Siva and Shakti into which all duality dissolved, and out of which all creation emerged. A ninth-century text, the *Chandamaharosana Tantra*, which translates as *The Great Moon Elixir*, encouraged the Tantric disciple to meditate and visualize alchemical transformation within himself as he engaged in sexual ritual. One of its suggested lovemaking positions, known as "the tantric tortoise," is combined with visualization to open up the heart *chakra* to the energy of universal compassion. The heart *chakra*, which is the fourth *chakra* on the etheric plane, is the place of union and integration between the bodily instincts and spiritual consciousness. This posture is moved into easily from one where the woman has been resting a leg upon her lover's shoulder. She then places both feet on her partner's chest so that the soles are laid over his

In the position of 'the tantric tortoise', the man employs breathing and visualisation techniques to control the release of his semen, transforming his orgasm into an energy of divine love.

185

heart centre. He should then squeeze her knees between his arms so that her thighs tighten and her *yoni* firmly clasps his *lingam*. As his sexual arousal increases with his movements, the man concentrates on his breathing techniques to control his semen, and to draw his orgasmic energy up through his body towards his heart centre.

In transcendental lovemaking you should use only positive images or visualizations, which by their nature will increase your reverence for your partner and allow your love energy to flow more freely.

Orgasmic energy

There are certain yoga techniques which enable a man to control his orgasmic reflexes during coitus so that his vital energy can be conserved and used for inner transformation. These practices, which are a combination of postures, muscular contractions, and breathing techniques, should be learnt under the proper guidance of an accomplished Tantric or yoga teacher. By abstaining or delaying his ejaculation, the man can also prolong his lovemaking to ensure that the woman is fully sexually satisfied.

When a man is concerned only with orgasm, either his own or his partner's, he is probably engaged in too much effort. He easily becomes depleted after he has ejaculated. He may even feel that he has lost something of himself, and Tantric teaching would agree that he has indeed leaked away some of his vital energy. Orgasm in itself is not to be rejected, for it can be the ecstatic pinnacle

of lovemaking. However, in Trantric thought, it is the control of the semen and the use of orgasmic energy as a force for transformation of consciousness that is important to the sexual and spiritual union of the man and woman. Tantra is less concerned about the female orgasm, if the woman does not lose energy by attaining to it. Many women are multi-orgasmic, and increase in vigour with each new climax.

When you are experimenting with transcendental sexuality, do not make an issue out of orgasm either one way or the other. If it happens anyway, then celebrate it fully, surrendering yourselves into its pleasurable sensations. However, try to find ways in which to extend the plateau phase of your lovemaking. As the woman, you can help your partner moderate his passion and slow down his lovemaking. Be aware of his arousal responses and recognize the moments when you should change from activity to stillness. It is important that your partner does not become sexually stimulated beyond his point of inevitability, when the orgasmic contractions begin in his prostate area, and he no longer has any control over semen emission. He must

Slow the pace of your lovemaking whenever sexual arousal becomes too intense so that your bodies and minds fall back into harmony with one another.

learn to slow down well before he reaches his peak of arousal. If you breathe together, keep eye contact, remain meditative and assume specific intimate but non-arousing coital positions, such as lying side-by-side in motionless conjugal embrace or in the spoons position, where you are curled with your back into your partner's body, your sexual responses will naturally adjust so that your lovemaking gains a timeless dimension.

Pure energy

Unlock your orgasmic energy from your genital area, drawing it up towards the crown of your head with visualizations, breathing, and concentration so that it sears through the whole of your body. Feel as if your bodies are pure energy and every cell is vibrating. Imagine that your physical boundaries are melting and that the two of you are merging together as one. Absorb your man into the depth of your being as if you are reclaiming your male half,

and yield your female energy to him so he can become united with his female side. Let your dualities dissolve into a spiritual union beyond the limits of your individual egos. Assume the Tantric *yab-yum* sexual position, where you are seated in coitus upon the lap of your lover, body to body and equal in posture. This is the Tantric posture of high union – the experience of cosmic bliss. Embrace closely, rocking gently, and if you desire, allow the orgasmic energy to explode ecstatically within you.

Become the goddess

Be empowered in your womanhood when making love to your man. Become like the consorts of the Tantric god Siva, whose diverse feminine natures were manifested in many forms. Celebrate the creative sexual power of your Shakti energy, and be wild and uncensored like the terrifying goddess Kali, or sweet and surrendering like Siva's wife, Parvati, who, according to Hindu mythology, made love with her Lord for one thousand years without interruption. Teach your partner to be unafraid of your sexuality and to experience its transforming force. Be the goddess of love, and take your man with you beyond the ordinary to discover the mysteries of transcendental sexuality.

Transcendental lovemaking transforms sexual energy into a communion of mind, body and spirit when conducted by the man and woman in an atmosphere of meditation and love.

Left: the embrace of 'yab-yum' is revered in tantric lovemaking as the sexual position of the highest form of union.

A

affection, physical 86–119
anal sex 159–160, 162
Ananga Ranga 183–184
aphrodisiacs 23, 24
Aquarius 80
Aries 76
arousal
    female 106
    foreplay 52, 86, 88,
        103–107, 182
    physiology of 65, 67
    sexual 22, 65
art
    erotic, Hindu 12–13, 15
    life studies 11
Artha 10
astrological compatibility
    74–83
astrology 74
attraction 48
Auparishtaka 148–158
autoeroticism 33–34

B

bathing, and intercourse 38,
    166
beauty 26–29
bi–sexuality 165
birth charts 74–75
Birth of Venus 87
biting 100, 102, 162
blood pressure 65
Blow of the Boar 128
"blow–job" 140, 148
body image 26
body language 43–44
bondage 165
Botticelli 87, *88*
bowed posture *177*
brain function, and essential
    oils 24
Burton, Sir Richard 14

C

Cancer (astrology) 77
Capricorn 80
chakras 171, 185
Chandamaharosana Tantra 185
circulation 24, 29, 65
    and orgasm 34
Clasping and Pressing
    position 58, 123–124, 139
cleansing 31

clitoris
clitoris
    masturbation 33
    and orgasm 8, 63
    stimulation 56, 63, 124,
        136–137, 148, 156
coitus 67
colours, and mood 37
communication 88, 178–179
compatibility
    astrological 74–83
    orgasmic 62, 64
    sexual 46–71, 95
condoms 14, 160
The Congress of a Cow 147–148
The Congress of the Crow 150,
    158
contraception
    condoms 14
    pill 8
    responsibility for 14
Cosmic Consciousness 11–12,
    170
Cosmic Creation 12
counseling 70–71
courtship 40–45
cunnilingus 148, 155–158

D

decor 37
Dharma 10
diet, healthy 22, 28–29
dimensions of genitals 52–54,
    58, 125, 126
domination 162

E

ejaculation 62, 65, 67–68, 152
    delayed 186
    premature 62, 67, 71
embracing 89–93
emotions, healing 24
empowerment 188
energy
    centres 171, 185
    orgasmic 184, 185, 186–188
    pure energy 187–188
equality 18
eroticism
    autoeroticism 33–34
    Eastern 8
    erotic acts 144–167
    female 33–34
    see also fantasy
essential oils 24–26, 31, 32, 37,
    38, 115, 182

exercise
exercise 28–29, 124
    pelvic floor 34, 129
exfoliation 29
eye contact 20, 43, 107

F

facial care 31, 96
family responsibilities 10, 18
fantasy 165, 166, 185
    masturbation 34
feet, care of 32, 111
fellatio 148–154
female
    arousal 106
    sexuality 8, 12, 18, 52, 134,
        170, 188
fitness 29
food
    healthy 28–29
    sensual 22
foreplay 52, 86, 88, 103–107,
    182
frigidity 25

G

G–spot 137
Gemini 76–77
gender roles 43
genitals, dimensions of 52–54,
    58, 125, 126
goals of life, Eastern 9–12
goddess of love 188
The Great Moon Elixir 185
group sex 165

H

hair care 31
hands, care of 32
healing 24, 107–108
health
    and lifestyle 28–29
    sexual 14
hearing 18–19
    sounds of love–making
        139, 141
heart rate 65
hepatitis B 160
Heterosexuality 64
"high union" 53–54, 56, 124,
    188
"highest union" 54
Hindu
    art 12–13, 15
    mythology 188

see also Shakti; Shiva
Pantheon 10
Tantra *see* Tantra
HIV/AIDS 14, 160
the home 34–38
horoscopes 76–83
hygiene 95, 158, 160

I

impotence 25, 71
incompatibility, sexual 69–71
intercourse *see* sexual
    intercourse

J

Javateshtika 91
Johnson, Virginia 8

K

Kali *137*, 188
    energy 134–136
Kama 9, 10–12
Kama Sastra Society 14
The Kama Sutra 8–9, 12, 14
keeping fit 29
Kinsey, Dr Alfred 8
kissing 88, 89, 93–99
Krishna *164*
Kshiraniraka 93
Kundalindi 171–173

L

Leo 77, *78*
libido
    enhancement of 24
    low 60–61
    male 58
Libra 79
lingam 12, 53, 179
listening skills 19
Lotus-like Position 175–176
love 52, 122, 188
love bites 100
"low union" 53–54, 58
lubrication 160, 162
    vaginal 64, 65, 67

M

"Mare's position" 34, 58, 129
Mars 81–83
massage 20, 24, 31, 52, 71, 89,
    107–119

facial 31
  techniques 115–119
Master, William 8
Masters and Johnson 8, 64, 65, 71
masturbation 33–34
meditation 178–179
Moksha 9
mood 24, 67
  and colours 37
"mouth congress" *see* oral sex

N

nerves, nerve endings 19, 123
networking 40
The nominal congress 151

O

oils 24–26, 31, 32, 37, 38, 115, 182
oral sex 148–158
orgasm
  compatibility 62, 64
  female 8, 62, 64–69
    and circulation 34
    multi–orgasm 8, 64
  male 62, 65, 67–68, 71
  orgasmic energy 184, 185, 186–188

P

pain 162
The Pair of Tongs position 138
Parvati 188
passion, degrees of 60
passivity 8, 52
pelvic floor, exercise 34, 129
penetration 88
  deep 56
  see also high union
penis
  dimensions of 52–53, 55, 56, 58, 125, 126
  in Indian art 12
  thrusting 129–132
  see also fallatio; lingam; sexual positions
performance anxiety 65
pheromones 23
physical affection 86–119
"piercing embrace" 44
Pisces 80
plants, choice of 23

plateau phase 66
"pleasure dome" 36
positions 34, 54–59, 123–129, 132–139, 144–148, 173–176, 183–184
premature ejaculation 62, 67, 71
Pressed position *59*, 126, 128
  Half pressed 126, 128
Pressing Position 124
prostate gland 67, 160, 162
psychosexual problems 70–71

R

relationships
  looking for 38–39
  quality of 10, 86, 176–182
  survival of 50
  see also compatibility; physical affection
relaxation 26, 108
Rising position 56, *57*, 124

S

sado–masochism 162
safer sex 14, 160
Sagittarius 79–80, *81*
scents 23
Scorpio 79
scratching 100–102, 162
scrotum 154
self esteem 26, 39, 108
Sensate Focus 71
the senses 18–23
sensuality
  female 12, 14
    sensory enhancement 18–26
  maintaining 88–89
  sensual foreplay 103–107
sex therapy 70–71
sexual boundaries 61–62
sexual compatibility 46–71, 95
  problems with 69–71
sexual dysfunction 69–71
  see also premature ejaculation; vaginismus
sexual experimentation 50
sexual healing 24–25
sexual intercourse
  duration 62
  location 166–167, 180
  performance anxiety 65
  positions 34, 54–59, 123–129, 132–139, 144–148, 173–176,

183–184
sexual response, phases of 65–69
sexual technique, male 8
sexual tension 25
sexuality
  bi–sexuality 165
  female 8, 12, 18, 52, 134, 170, 188
  male 52
  transcendental 170–189
sexually transmitted diseases 14, 160, 166
Shakti 12, 185, 188
"shampooing" *see* massage
sight 20
Siva 12, 151, 185, 188
Sixty Nine 150, 158
skin 19
  care of 29–32
  see also massage
smell 22–23, 95
  aromatic essences 23–26
social life 38–40
sounds of love–making 139, 141
spices 24
spiritual life 10, 170
  healing 24
Splitting a Bamboo Position 174
Standing position 144, 167
submission 162
Sun signs 75–82
Superior position 56, 134–139
Supported Congress 144, 167
Suspended Congress 146, 167
Sutra 9
Suvarnabha 166
The Swing position 138
Synastry 83

T

taboo 166
Tantra 11–12, 148, 170–173
  Tantric colours 37
  Tantric sexual rituals 22, 23, 151, 182–188
  Tantric texts 25, 52, 62, 174
  "the tantric tortoise" 185
Taoist texts 52, 62, 170
taste *21*, 22, 95
Taurus 75, 76
tension 96
The Congress of the Bulls 166
The Congress of the Cows 166
threesomes 165

thrusting 129–132
Tila–tandulaka 92
tolerance, relationships 50
The Top *133*
The Top position 138
touch 19–20, 44–45, 86–88
  see also massage
"touching embrace" 45
transcendental sexuality 170–189
Turning Position 173
Twining Position 124, *125*

U

Union of the beast and birds 146–147
United Congress 165
universal compassion 185

V

vagina 53–56, 58, 123
  G–spot 137
  lubrication 64, 65, 67
  see also cunnilingus; genitals; sexual positions; yoni
Vaginismus 71
Vatsayana 8, 14, 52
Vedic tradition 74
venereal diseases 14
  see also sexually transmitted diseases
Venus 81–83
virginity, female 43
Virgo 77, 79
visualization 185–186
Vrikshadhirudhaka 91–92
vulva 137, 148, 174
  in Indian art 12, *13*

W

water, lovemaking in 166–167
Widely opened position 55
Wife of Indra position 56
Woman on Top 132–139

Y

Yawning position 56, 124, 126–127, 174
yoga 124, 172–173, *175*
yoni 12, 53, 94, 155, 174, 179
  power *see* Mare's position
  see also vagina

Acknowledgements

Commissioned drawings by Stuart Miller

Photographs (with page references) from:

AKG London: 157 (Jean-Louis Nou)

Art Archive: 72 (British Library), 75 and 78 (Bibliotheque Nationale, Paris), 81 (Glasgow University Library), 82–83 (National Gallery, London, Eileen Tweedy), 87 (Galleria degli Offizi, Florence, Dagli Orti), 90 (Victoria and Albert Museum, London, Eileen Tweedy), 153 (JFB), 181 (Victoria and Albert Museum, London)

Chrysalis Images: 49, 66, 189, 95, 109, 110, 113, 114, 116, 167

Image Bank: 28 (P. Ridenour), 41 (Romilly Lockyer), 103 (David de Lossy), 104 (Donata Pizzi), 118 (Wayne H. Chasan)

Manya Igel Arts Ltd: 11

Mary Evans Picture Library: 27, 171 (from the book *Theosobia Practica*)

Special Photogaphers Library: 16 (Marianne Morris), 25 (Brian Jacquest), 33 (Anne Leigniel), 37 (Ouka Lee), 51 and 61 (Joyce Tenneson), 84 (Tania Hirshbell), 163 (Klanger & Boink)

Stock Market: 21 (Thomas Schweizer), 53 (Steve Prezant), 63 (Larry Williams), 93 (Jan Feingersh '97)

Trip/Dinodia: 46 (Sun Temple, Konarak), 145, 161, 164

Werner Forman Archive: 2, 6, 13 and 15 (De Young Museum), 35 (India Office Library, London), 135, 120, 125, 127, 130, 131, 133, 140, 146, 149, 168 (Philip Goldman Collection, London), 172, 175, 177, 178